MASTERING WEALTH

VOLUME 2 PURPOSE

PERCY "MASTER P" MILLER

Plus Insights From 20 Thought Leaders & Experts

"Mastering wealth begins with mastering your purpose."

– Percy "Master P" Miller

TABLE OF PURPOSE

MASTERING WEALTH: VOLUME 2 PURPOSE INTRODUCTION

Mastering Wealth: Volume 2 Purpose takes readers on a journey into the heart of building wealth with intention. It moves beyond the surface-level definitions of financial success, focusing instead on the intersection of wealth, purpose, and legacy. This volume combines the insights and strategies of seasoned experts and thought leaders, each contributing their unique perspective to inspire and guide readers on their financial and personal journeys.

The book emphasizes that wealth is not merely about accumulating money but also about creating opportunities, building legacies, and fostering meaningful impact. It begins by exploring the role of philanthropy and the responsibility of using wealth to give back to communities. Highlighting the importance of generosity and social responsibility encourages readers to align their financial goals with values that contribute to the greater good.

The purpose of branding is presented as an essential aspect of wealth-building, illustrating how individuals can harness their brilliance to create lasting impressions and opportunities. Through lessons in strategic positioning, readers are shown how to amplify their unique talents and ideas to stand out in competitive markets.

One of the book's key themes is using resources like life insurance and other financial tools to secure long-term stability and generational wealth. The chapters delve into actionable steps for leveraging these tools, offering practical advice on protecting assets, building equity, and creating sustainable income streams.

The book also delves into emotional and psychological aspects of wealth, such as curbing emotional spending and cultivating resilience. It acknowledges the challenges and sacrifices inherent in pursuing financial success and guides managing fear, overcoming setbacks, and staying focused on long-term goals. Through personal stories and expert insights, readers are encouraged to face their vulnerabilities and grow stronger through adversity.

Education and community are also central themes. The book emphasizes the importance of training the next generation to succeed financially and become leaders and changemakers. It explores how investments in education, particularly Black-owned K-12 institutions, and programs that train youth as healers and innovators, can empower communities and break cycles of poverty.

Real estate and digital marketing are presented as powerful vehicles for scaling businesses and creating wealth. Chapters dedicated to building generational wealth through real estate teach readers how to strategically invest in properties and use them as tools for financial independence and community revitalization. Similarly, exploring digital marketing showcases how leveraging technology can connect businesses to broader audiences and drive rapid growth.

At its core, *Mastering Wealth* is a guide to purposeful living through wealth creation. It challenges readers to think beyond personal gain, encouraging them to focus on legacy-building and the transformative power of their financial decisions. Combining actionable strategies with deeper introspection, the book equips readers to approach wealth-building as a means to an end and a journey toward a meaningful and impactful life.

This book is more than a roadmap for financial success—it is a call to action for individuals to align their wealth with their values, leave an enduring legacy, and make a difference in the world. Whether you're just starting your financial journey or looking to elevate your impact, *Mastering Wealth* offers the tools and insights to help you achieve your goals while staying true to your purpose.

STAY COMMITTED!

Percy Miller

THE PURPOSE OF PHILANTHROPY

"Philanthropy is the bridge that connects our blessings to those in need, reminding us that our greatest wealth is in our ability to give." - Percy Miller

Percy "Master P" Miller

Philanthropy in Mastering Wealth

Philanthropy holds great power to create lasting impact, shaping lives and communities for the better. For over 30 years, I have dedicated myself to this principle. I am humbled to have received national recognition for my efforts, including awards from the NAACP and keys to various cities. These honors symbolize more than personal accolades—they represent the lives changed, and communities uplifted through the work I've been privileged to do. Each recognition serves as a reminder that true success is measured by personal achievements and the positive change we inspire in others.

To me, philanthropy is not just about financial contributions—it is a foundational aspect of true wealth. It connects us, fosters meaningful transformation, and solidifies the legacy we leave behind. It is an investment in the future, one that pays dividends through healthier, more resilient people and communities. My commitment to philanthropy goes beyond giving money; it includes dedicating time, energy, and resources to create opportunities for growth and help people break free from cycles of poverty.

The Ripple Effect of Breaking Cycles

Philanthropy can disrupt systemic barriers and break generational cycles of inequality. When these cycles are broken, individuals who once faced insurmountable obstacles begin recognizing their potential. They transform into agents of change within their communities, stepping into leadership roles and inspiring others. This transformation creates a ripple effect, touching families, neighborhoods, and entire communities.

As these empowered individuals address local challenges, they contribute to long-term improvements in education, healthcare, and economic activity. Resilient communities emerge, offering a foundation for future generations to thrive. By challenging inequality and fostering inclusion, philanthropy doesn't just create immediate change—it builds a more equitable society and strengthens the economy for the benefit of all.

The Philosophy of Giving

Philanthropy is a guiding principle in my life. It's not about writing checks; it's about creating programs that tackle root causes and uplift those who need it most—whether young people stepping into adulthood or older people who paved the way for us. I believe true wealth isn't measured by what I have but by what I give.

No matter how small, each act of giving holds the power to inspire others to do the same. I intentionally invest in the most profound and lasting impact areas, such as education, entrepreneurship, and economic empowerment. Through scholarships, youth initiatives, or mental health programs, I see these investments as building blocks for a better future.

Impact Through Team Hope Foundation™

Central to my philanthropic efforts is the Team Hope Foundation™, an organization I founded to address critical educational, mental health, and wellness challenges. Team Hope's mission is to provide resources and support for young people and older people, ensuring they have the tools they need to succeed.

The foundation's scholarships open doors to higher education for those who might otherwise be unable to afford it. Mentorship programs guide the next generation, providing them with role models and opportunities. Community initiatives focus on wellness, offering tangible support to those in need. Team Hope has transformed countless lives and strengthened communities by empowering individuals and fostering growth.

The Wealth of Influence

One of the most important lessons I've learned through philanthropy is that true wealth is reflected in the well-being and prosperity of the communities we uplift. Success isn't defined by personal achievements alone but by how many others we lift as we rise. Philanthropy creates a continuous cycle of giving, inspiring others to act and make a positive difference in their communities.

No matter how small, each act of generosity can spark more significant change. In a world often filled with negativity, my goal is to be a light, igniting hope and inspiring action. Through my philanthropic efforts, I strive to create a legacy of wealth and meaningful change that uplifts individuals, empowers communities, and builds a better future for all.

This commitment to giving back defines my journey to mastering wealth. At its core, wealth is about creating opportunities, fostering resilience, and ensuring that the impact of what we do today resonates for generations to come. Through philanthropy, we can all achieve something more significant than personal success: a legacy of hope, empowerment, and transformation.

NOTES

NOTES

NOTES

NOTES

THE PURPOSE OF
BRANDING YOUR BRILLIANCE

When you understand the value of your name and actively embrace your unique talents and abilities, it becomes more than self-empowerment; it's a bold affirmation—a resounding "Yes" to God.
-Tiana Von Johnson

Tiana Von Johnson

Branding Your Brilliance

The journey of transforming your life through branding is about creating a powerful, distinctive personal identity that authentically represents who you are and what you stand for. For over a decade, this approach has changed my life and catapulted me into becoming an influential figure in business. Recognizing the value of my name and showcasing it in its truest form has been a cornerstone of my entrepreneurial success.

When you understand the value of your name and actively embrace your unique talents and abilities, it becomes more than self-empowerment; it's a bold affirmation—a resounding "Yes" to God that you are committed to using your gifts for meaningful and impactful purposes. This journey of branding your brilliance is about more than just personal growth; it's about aligning with your divine purpose. It's about acknowledging that your talents are not solely for your benefit but are meant to be shared with the world in ways that uplift and inspire. When you embrace your true calling and purpose, you enter a life of fulfillment, where personal achievements are more than just accolades—they become manifestations of a higher calling. Every level of success is a testament to your commitment to living out your divine purpose and contributing positively to the world.

The Opportunity Mindset

Throughout my entrepreneurial journey, I have remained dedicated to showcasing my own brilliance while helping others discover theirs. This mindset has become the cornerstone of my millionaire philosophy, driving me to continuously recalibrate, invest in self-improvement, and create opportunities for myself and others. Although I sometimes fell short, I pushed through every storm with renewed determination.

It is a fact that more millionaires are born during times of crisis than in periods of stability, highlighting a fundamental truth: opportunities exist in every season, even in the darkest moments. The key is having the right mindset—seeing beyond distractions and fear. The opportunity mindset separates those who achieve success from those who don't. As you brand your brilliance, this mindset becomes crucial. You must activate your "opportunity radar" and remain open to new possibilities. Each opportunity you seize brings you closer to your goals and expands your growth potential.

The Power of Your Name

One of the most powerful aspects of branding is the influence of your name. When you elevate your name and fully embrace its potential, you create a foundation that allows everything you touch to thrive. Take, for example, how the Kardashians have mastered this concept. Their name alone opens doors and creates opportunities for ventures in various industries. While you may have a different level of recognition, you can adopt this strategy by ensuring that your name stands for something meaningful. Your name can become a powerful brand that propels everything you do forward.

Strategies to Be the Brand

Once you've discovered your purpose and successfully branded your name, the next step is to create businesses and opportunities that align with your brand. Think about what you envision for yourself within this brand—perhaps becoming a speaker, an author, a coach, or launching products that reflect your identity. Your brand should represent the essence of who you are and serve the needs of your audience. Every move you make should build upon your brand, adding layers of success that contribute to your legacy.

Branding with Purpose

As I close this chapter, I must share that branding your brilliance goes far beyond self-promotion—embracing your divine purpose, recognizing your unique gifts, and sharing them with the world. Doing so creates a lasting legacy, inspiring others to discover their brilliance and transforming lives. Through perseverance, self-reliance, and an opportunity mindset, you can elevate your name, build successful ventures, and create a brand that resonates with purpose and impact.

Take a sneak peek at my book, *"7 Laws of Entrepreneurial Success: The Millionaire Mind Manifesto,"* which will help you sharpen your mind to master wealth.

NOTES

NOTES

NOTES

BONUS SNEAK PEEK

We are excited to offer a sneak peek into Dr. Tiana Von Johnson's book, *"7 Laws of Entrepreneurial Success: The Millionaire Mind Manifesto!"* For over 15 years, Tiana Von Johnson, a partner and close associate of our visionary author Percy Miller, has shared powerful principles that have guided countless individuals toward success. Her transformative journey, marked by triumphs, setbacks, and essential lessons, laid the groundwork for her previous works, "Mindset Makeover" and "Million Dollar Mindset," culminating in this latest edition.

In this book, Tiana explores her journey from an impoverished upbringing in the Bronx to becoming an entrepreneurial powerhouse. Each law promotes personal discovery, resilience, and the cultivation of a millionaire mindset, encouraging readers to break free from self-imposed limitations. These seven transformative laws offer practical advice, making this book a manifesto for anyone committed to seizing control of their destiny and building a lasting legacy.

BEARING FRUIT IN HARD SOIL

Stories, Blessings, and Lessons: My Impoverished Family Line Resilient Roots in the Concrete Jungle

From as early as I can remember, I refused to settle or be another forgotten seed in the hard soil of an impoverished landscape. My path is one of breaking barriers, defying societal norms, and rejecting the limitations imposed by others. Rooted in the conviction that every individual can flourish, regardless of their family line, I have grown resilient against the odds. I am against stagnant mindsets and outdated systems – the rocky ground threatening growth. I despise watching people live beneath their true potential, wilting in the shadows of what could be. My existence serves as a catalyst for progress, nurturing and pushing people to rise above their current circumstances, often exceeding even their wildest dreams. Those who cling to the comfort of mediocrity may find themselves at odds with me. I am committed to cultivating a garden of excellence, even in the harshest of soils.

Foundation for Growth

I've learned that true strength is not just about thriving in adversity but transforming it into a foundation for growth. Just as the most challenging terrains can yield the most resilient plants, my challenges have become the nutrients for my unyielding spirit. Every obstacle I encountered in the landscape of my life has been a lesson in perseverance, teaching me the art of turning barren ground into fertile land. My mission extends beyond my success; it's about sowing seeds of ambition and hope in others, guiding them to tap into their potential. This is not just a personal triumph but a communal uprising, where success is not measured by escaping the hard soil but by enriching it, ensuring that those who come after me find a land more conducive to their dreams.

Growing Up

As a child growing up in the Bronx, New York, I was born into a life designed to keep people stagnant and reliant on the 'system.' I faced trials and hardships as my mother struggled with mental health issues and depression, relying on public assistance to make ends meet. There were no silver spoons, no inheritances, no influential mentors, no family-owned business handed down, no generational wealth transfer, no conversations of wealth around the dinner table, and no connections to offer me an easier life. Nobody was coming to save me; I only had hopes, dreams, and ambitions.

I have always boldly proclaimed my desire for success. I embodied the essence of a boss, mimicking a 'businesswoman' by carrying a briefcase to school instead of a book bag. I set up a desk in my room with a calculator, pens, notepad, and a makeshift computer because my parents couldn't afford to buy me one. I even asked my father to take me to the post office to collect a batch of their forms so I could have them on my desk, mimicking the appearance of a real 'work' desk. I envisioned myself amassing great wealth and was determined to embark on this journey, regardless of the challenges I might face. Wrestling with adversity and nurturing dreams of success became second nature to me.

From Risk to Reward

Throughout my life, I've demonstrated a propensity for taking risks, firmly believing that playing it safe was part of my family DNA but not mine. To me, playing it safe resembled resigning to a life of blandness, which to me was like consuming unseasoned food—it may sustain you, but it lacks the flavor of true fulfillment. Each risk was a step out of my comfort zone, a conscious choice to actively pursue my goals instead of remaining stagnant. This approach honed my resilience and provided opportunities that a cautious approach would never have manifested. The risks I embraced, some good and others not so good, were the spices that added depth and excitement to the journey, transforming my life into a vibrant series of experiences and achievements.

My Father, The Record Man

Despite feeling embarrassed about my impoverished family line, my mother's reliance on public assistance, and my father's hustler mentality, I am deeply grateful to both of them. Unbeknownst to me, they played a pivotal role in my life, serving as two of my most influential teachers and sowing seeds that have shaped the mindset I possess today. I worked alongside my father, affectionately known as King George, the local record man and DJ, hustling records on the bustling streets of Harlem. Through this experience, I absorbed valuable lessons in negotiation and business, further igniting my passion for entrepreneurship.

My Mother, Magic Fingers

At the same time, my mother's diverse creative pursuits, including cosmetology, sewing, cooking, crafting, and floral design, nurtured my innate creative genius. She was affectionately known by the nickname 'Cookie,' but many people referred to her as "Magic Fingers" because of her exceptional skills with her hands. By melding the entrepreneurial and creative talents inherited from both my parents, I cultivated a creatively unique and ambitious mindset, but there was so much more I needed to learn.

Navigating My Identity

Throughout my childhood, I encountered challenges I never discussed. I was born with my father's green eyes, sandy blond hair, and very fair skin—starkly contrasting my parents' caramel complexions. These features, ironically, became a source of hardship. At school, I was targeted by darker-skinned girls who accused me of 'trying to be white' or for believing 'I was better than them.' This led to constant bullying and exclusion from various groups and activities, fueled by a deep-seated hatred towards my appearance and complexion. I often found myself trying to tan my skin or contemplating wearing contacts to hide my actual eye color in hopes of gaining acceptance.

In addition, I had blotches and freckles on my face, which heightened my insecurities. Moreover, my aunt enrolled me in school early, making me younger than my peers. Consequently, while all my friends were experiencing their menstrual cycles, mine did not arrive until years later. I found myself lying about my age, pretending we were all the same age. Feeling lost and left behind, accepting my appearance and internal struggles became a significant challenge, especially when facing hostility from fellow Black girls.

Navigating Through Shadows

The challenges of bullying did not end with my childhood; instead, they extended into my adult life. Many women opted not to work with me, perceiving me as someone who thinks 'I'm all that." To some, this may appear minor, but its impact on my personal and professional life was profound, often casting a shadow over my achievements due to the insecurities of others. Faced with a choice—to cultivate resilience or to remain weighed down by bullying, jealousy, and negativity—I chose the former.

With time, I committed to embracing my true self and shielding myself from harsh judgments. I mastered the art of standing firm in adversity and creating distance from those unwilling to confront their own issues. This journey of self-discovery and resilience highlighted the importance of protecting my energy and staying focused on my path, regardless of the obstacles posed by others.

Life from Two Perspectives

Have you ever wondered why some people rise above their circumstances and succeed while others are forced to live below the surface of life? We all have personal struggles, but some of us make bad decisions or settle into a life where bad decisions are our only choice. However, I learned that no matter how you grew up, you are not a product of your circumstances; you are a product of your decisions because you get to choose another path. If you cannot control your decisions, you cannot control your life.

Growing up was challenging. Poverty surrounded me, and the majority of people I knew followed the conventional path in life. It seemed like the world was telling me this would be my permanent reality everywhere I turned, and I despised that idea. The fear of ending up with nothing and living an ordinary life filled me with dread and anxiety. It was a constant battle to break free from this cycle.

Two Dreamers: Nicole and Me

My best friend Nicole and I shared a desire for more in life. We were just two young girls attending CIS 229 junior high school, diligently trying to figure out how to realize our dreams. With bright ideas and big hopes, we actively engaged in dance classes and coordinated the school's fashion and dance shows. We weren't mischievous, nor did we engage in reckless behavior; all we wanted was to be businesswomen and continue dreaming. However, in our final year of school, Nicole's mother passed away, and her father moved them out of state. We didn't have cell phones then, so I had no way to contact her. I was left alone and heartbroken because my best friend was gone. Who would I share my dreams with now?

Over the next few years, I couldn't shake the rebellious feeling that came with losing Nicole, my 'dream' partner. However, my unwavering determination to stay the course overpowered any inclination not to do so. I knew Nicole would be pursuing her dreams, and in a way, I still felt connected to her, understanding that I should be on a similar path. With this in mind, I began selling records with my father on 125th Street and assisting him at his record conventions. I also helped my mother sell her dolls and crocheted blankets in front of my grandmother's house. My journey towards entrepreneurship was in full swing.

Rejecting the Trapped Mindset

I realized that successful people understood something I had yet to grasp fully. That was the moment I started asking the right questions, and in doing so, I began to find the answers. It became evident to me that the world has two predominant mindsets. The first is the 'trapped or fixed' mindset, where individuals accept their circumstances, adhering to the prescribed 'system' or life's established norms. These minds believe that they can only achieve what's within their current 'ability' or 'power' to attain.

The other mindset is the 'growth or free' mindset. Those who possess it forge their path, rejecting that their potential is confined to what they already know. Instead, they seek constant growth, evolution, and development. Unfortunately, many people live with a trapped or fixed mindset. They grapple with financial struggles, overwhelming debt, and stress because they can't seem to find a way out of their current circumstances. They react to life rather than creating the life they desire. I've experienced and had both mindsets firsthand.

The System Has Failed You

The system couldn't have failed you in many ways, but for many, it has. New generations of retirees face the harsh reality that their struggles will only intensify each year. I have a friend who spent 30 years working for a significant company, only to retire and get a job at Walmart to make ends meet. This underscores how individuals can dedicate themselves to a career for decades only to still encounter financial difficulties in retirement, despite their loyalty and commitment.

With that said, it's crucial to recognize that you possess power within your mind that far exceeds what you've imagined. Realizing your full potential is one of the many goals that lead to spiritual fulfillment, emotional well-being, and mental happiness. Everyone is born with a mind ideally suited to meet their unique needs, but the choice is yours to unlock that potential. I discovered I could achieve more than I had ever dreamed possible by being proactive, taking action, and positioning myself where I needed to be. I let go of certain friends and separated myself from family members who were stuck. When my mindset shifted, my life shifted, and I was able to free myself from the trap and embrace the power within.

Embracing Your Personal Potential

I believe that God has blessed every one of us with the personal potential to be exactly who we want to be. Life is just a process of finding out who or what that is. There is a formula that results in success, but it does not exist in the external world. It starts, plays, and finishes in your mind. What you believe right now makes up who you are. Belief dictates what we think and thought and dictates how we behave. You must start with your mind if you want your behavior to change.

Think of it this way—there is a very good reason you go to work every day. You acknowledge the necessity of a paycheck, and you understand that working is the means to obtain one. You summon the energy to head to work every morning, dedicating your day to securing your income. This process is rooted in the belief that diligent work will lead to financial stability. There's an unspoken promise of a brighter future. However, let's contemplate an alternative perspective—things may not improve as expected. What if I could prove that dedicating your entire career to your current job won't necessarily guarantee you financial success and happiness? The truth is, deep down inside, you already know this.

To read more, order now on Amazon or visit TianaVonJohnson.com.

NOTES

NOTES

NOTES

THE PURPOSE OF PASSION

Dr. Vicki Wright Hamilton

The Purpose of Passion

Passion is one of the most incredible forces in the world, and it can shape every aspect of our lives. Over your lifetime, when you discover your passion, it can impact your mental and physical health, mindset, ability to face life's challenges, and, most of all, your joy. I want to share how your passion can multiply your benefits and lead to a more fulfilled and resilient life. When you embrace your passion, you reap numerous benefits, the most immediate of which is the increased joy it brings to your life. When you love what you do, your tasks become a new source of fulfillment. This joy is not fleeting but becomes a consistent part of your life, becoming a positive force that drives your well-being.

Early on in my career, two experiences opened me up to my passion for technology. The first was in the banking industry, where my main position included running a proof operator machine (where checks are coded). The second was when I had the opportunity to assist my mother with data collection for her dissertation. Although very different, these early work experiences served as the catalyst for my passion for the ever-growing technological landscape. Ultimately, it helped me realize that I enjoyed data, technology, and business; I wasn't quite mature enough to understand precisely what that meant or where it would lead, but I knew I had to pursue this passion further.

Exposing myself early on to work that aligned with my purpose brought immense happiness to my life. It gave me the strength to navigate personal and professional hurdles with a new sense of clarity. I'd even go as far as to say it showed me that it is possible to "never work a day in your life." Instead, the key to success here is to welcome work that creates a sense of fulfillment. Numerous studies have indicated that higher levels of happiness and satisfaction come when individuals engage in activities they are passionate about. Imagine a world where every task has the potential to become meaningful. The passion you've cultivated throughout your life aligns your work with your interests and values, producing a feeling of meaningfulness with each task presented.

It's important to note that adapting your mindset is crucial to this journey. A clear mindset can help you strive and succeed in your goals and the entire journey. Exuding passion in every step of your journey inherently becomes just as rewarding as the end goal. This intrinsic perspective has the potential to keep you committed and engaged, even when things are not aligned as previously envisioned. It's this fulfillment that provides an infinite source of energy and enthusiasm.

The Art of the Possible

When you embrace your passions fully, it has the potential to create a mindset of endless possibilities. You feel so comfortable in your journey that you can begin challenging the status quo and envisioning new opportunities and ideas. This forward-thinking way can be described as "the art of the possible." It's the ability to visualize beyond what is in front of you and imagine what could be achieved. This perspective drives innovation and creativity, creating a sense of purpose and direction.

Reflecting on my journey, I took many strategic risks and pursued various ambitious goals due to my ability to see the potential in my work. This approach was crucial for my success, professionally and personally. It made me feel comfortable pushing the boundaries and exploring more innovative ideas. My passion for technology ignited a sense of curiosity in me that I didn't know could exist.

Working to Live, Not Living to Work

Another substantial benefit of embracing your passion is the dynamic way of shifting your perspective, once again, from "living to work" to "working to live." Looking forward to your work, day in and day out, comes when you're passionate about your work. Creating this mental shift is crucial for achieving a healthy work-life balance, making it something you look forward to daily. When your passion is engaged, the sense of accomplishment you feel from your work extends into your personal life. Creating this continuous stream of joy and fulfillment indicates that you still carry that positive mindset and energy even when not working.

As a strategic business coach, I've witnessed this transformation in many clients. The pattern typically starts with them having a sense of overwhelm and burnout. Once I can work with them to uncover passions, their perspective shifts. They realize they can make work a source of joy rather than stress. They once again find themselves more energized and engaged in all their lives. This balance is not about attempting to divide your time equally between work and your personal life but about integrating the two in a way that both become fulfilling.

Embracing Change with Passion

Change can mainly be described as complex, but it's also an inevitable part of life. If you are passionate about what you do, I've found that you are better equipped to handle that change. In times of uncertainty, passion provides a stable foundation to help you adapt to new circumstances and find new opportunities. It aligns with our core motivations. We all have an internal "radio station" playing in our minds called W-I-I-FM, or "What's In It For Me." This metaphorical station represents our core desires and interests. We are more adaptable and resilient when we listen to this station and align our passions with our actions.

It's also essential to tune into others' radio stations. Understanding and empathizing with others' perspectives can enhance our own vision and help us grow. This allows us to integrate creative ideas into our own work and learn from differing viewpoints. This process can enrich our passion and foster professional and personal growth.

In moments of change, your passion acts as a life compass, guiding you through uncharted waters. It helps you stay focused on what truly matters most, even if that path seems impossible or unclear. Passion has the power to give you the courage to embrace change. To navigate it gracefully and confidently, seeing it as an opportunity rather than a threat is essential.

Growing Through Passion

Passion is described as dynamic and ever-changing, not static. We learn and grow, and we continuously want to have joy. The driving force of this growth is our intrinsic motivation to improve and excel in what we love. Passion allows us to strive for new skills and knowledge and explore new territories.

Passion allows us to connect with like-minded individuals, fostering a supportive network that promotes peer feedback, collaboration, and encouragement. It creates a community where we inspire and motivate one another to achieve greater success. Engaging with others who share our passions opens the door to exchanging ideas, gaining fresh perspectives, and cultivating deep friendships. In my experience, my passion for coaching has led me to remarkable individuals and lasting relationships. These connections have enriched my life profoundly, providing professional opportunities, personal support, and meaningful friendships. So, take a moment to explore your passions and embrace the journey of pursuing them without hesitation. Embrace, nurture, and allow it to lead you towards a life filled with joy and happiness.

About Dr. Vicki Wright Hamilton

Dr. Vicki Wright Hamilton is a seasoned strategic business and leadership coach and keynote speaker renowned for her empowering influence on entrepreneurs and corporate leaders for over 30 years. She has held C-suite and senior executive roles in the top 500 companies in technology and business, generating millions of dollars. Vicki has led technology companies to conceptualize, design, and execute innovative technology plans, yielding a $20M ROI. She expertly combines strategic planning with empathetic support to help entrepreneurs overcome challenges, clarify their goals, and accelerate growth. Her coaching methodology fosters confidence, innovation, and impactful decision-making tailored to her client's needs. Her mission is to equip entrepreneurs with the tools and mindset necessary for success, ensuring their ventures align with their vision and values.

As the CEO of VWH Consulting, a firm specializing in technology strategy, leadership, and business coaching, Vicki helps clients transform themselves and their businesses. Her unique GameFace™ methodology and inspirational journey as a Black woman in tech and business have made her a highly sought-after speaker, where she inspires and educates audiences on entrepreneurial support, leadership development, and digital innovation, emphasizing the integration of advanced technologies for business efficiency.

For more information, visit VickiWrightHamilton.com.

NOTES

NOTES

NOTES

THE PURPOSE OF LIFE INSURANCE

Tony R. Jackson
"The Real Money Coach"

Life insurance is a contract between an individual, the policyholder, and the insurance company where the insurer agrees to pay the designated beneficiary a sum of money upon the insured person's death in exchange for premium payments. This is very true, and it is what we traditionally thought life insurance to be. However, that's different from what this article is about. Now, I want to uphold the importance of life insurance. One of my most popular seminars is titled "Go-Fund-Me Ain't Life Insurance." Many people do not realize that more than 125,000 Go-Fund-Me's are started yearly to cover funeral expenses. Again, that is not what this article is about. In this article, I will give you five game-changing benefits you didn't know about life insurance outside of the traditional death benefit that comes to mind when we hear life insurance. This article is not about the policies our grandparents and others bought from the insurance agents who would come by the house and collect the money weekly. This article is about strategies available within life insurance that very few people know about or take advantage of. Now, let's dig into the five game-changing benefits of life insurance.

Purpose #1 – Generational Wealth

Although this relates to the death benefit, I wanted to start with generational wealth. Generational wealth has become a buzzword in our culture. Everybody is discussing creating generational wealth everywhere we turn, including social media. Life insurance is the most straightforward, effective, and affordable way to create generational wealth. Leveraging the cost of premiums to leave hundreds of thousands of dollars in benefits to our family, including our spouse, children, and grandchildren, is one of the most underutilized strategies in the Black community. We often think life insurance only covers funeral costs, but it's much more than that. It's a way to give the next generation a head start in building and maintaining wealth. The proceeds can be used to start a business, buy real estate, or invest. This is precisely why, for many years, black people were not permitted to own life insurance beyond small burial policies. Those burial policies often fell short of covering the actual funeral cost, which today can easily exceed $10,000 to $20,000. Life insurance allows us to leave millions of tax-free benefits to the next generation for pennies on the dollar.

Purpose #2 – Living Benefits

Over my 27-year career, I've seen the evolution of life insurance to include living benefits. These living benefits typically cover terminal, critical, and chronic illnesses. Not all insurance carriers and policies include these living benefits, but most offer some form of terminal illness benefit. The terminal illness benefit is paid when a doctor certifies that you have become terminally ill with a limited life expectancy. Less common are critical illness and chronic illness benefits. Critical illness benefits are paid when you have a significant medical condition like a heart attack, stroke, kidney failure, or cancer.

We know these medical conditions occur far too often in our communities. The key to receiving this benefit is that the medical condition negatively impacts your mortality. Chronic illness benefits, which are more common than critical, can vary between insurance companies. However, the conditions for activating the benefit are standard across the board. This benefit pays when you need help with two of the six daily activities of living: bathing, continence, dressing, eating, toileting, and transferring. It can also be paid if you have a cognitive disorder such as dementia or Alzheimer's disease.

Purpose #3 – Cash Value Accumulation

Many financial gurus in mainstream media promote term life insurance, often citing affordability as the primary reason. While term life insurance is the right choice for many people, it overlooks the tremendous benefits of cash value accumulation that are unavailable with term life insurance. Term life insurance covers you for a specific period, like 10 or 20 years, or until a certain age. Once the term expires, coverage ends, or the premiums become unaffordable. You are left with no life insurance or anything to show for the years of paying premiums.

On the other hand, permanent life insurance is designed to keep the same premium throughout the policy's life. There are two types of permanent life insurance: whole life and universal life. Both accumulate cash value, which can be used in various ways. I often compare it to home equity, which you might gain over time if you own a house. Like home equity, cash value can supplement retirement, pay for college, start a business, or invest in more assets. The unique feature of cash value is that it's easily accessible and doesn't require loan approval, credit checks, income verification, or repayment. Essentially, it functions like your own bank. If you need to start with term life insurance, there's no shame. Make sure it is convertible to permanent life insurance so you can upgrade to a permanent policy when possible.

Purpose #4 – Tax-Free Income

Although many people are becoming more familiar with the cash value benefits of permanent life insurance, including concepts like "be your own bank," "family bank," and "infinite banking" —thanks to social media. The average person still doesn't realize how powerful tax-free income can be in a financial plan. Saving on future taxes can be one of the greatest strategies to help you live your desired lifestyle. Tax-free income alone can increase your disposable cash by 25% to 40%. There are two primary ways permanent life insurance can provide tax-free income. The first is by making regular contributions to a permanent life insurance plan like an indexed universal or whole life policy. Over time, you'll accumulate cash value, which can function like a high-yield savings account and become a nontaxable income stream.

The second, less-known strategy is converting your current tax-qualified accounts, like 401(k), IRA, and TSP accounts, into a tax-free income using life insurance. Many people have heard about Roth conversions but need to be made aware of the benefits of using life insurance as a vehicle to convert these taxable accounts into tax-free ones. By utilizing a cash-value life insurance policy, these conversions offer all the benefits mentioned in this article and often require little to no out-of-pocket cash. You can also leverage the premiums to create a dual-purpose asset. In other words, the same money will work for you in multiple ways. I've used this concept to help my clients save millions in taxes and create millions in tax-free lifetime income.

Purpose #5 – Business Continuation

Life insurance is often used in business succession and continuation planning. One type is key person insurance, which provides financial protection if a key employee or business owner dies. It helps maintain the company's financial stability while adjusting to that person's loss. It also typically includes a portion of the death benefit payable to the employee's family. If cash-value life insurance is used, it also provides additional retirement funds to key employees.

Life insurance can also fund the buyout of an owner's share of the business in the event of death. This legal agreement, called a buy-sell agreement, prevents the remaining business owners from being forced to do business with the deceased owner's heirs, who may or may not have the business expertise or character to function as a business partner. It also provides income for the deceased owner's family, ensuring a smooth transition that keeps the business profitable and supports the deceased owner's family.

Final Thought

As you can see, life insurance has multiple uses beyond the traditional death benefit. It's much more than just a payout when you're gone. I encourage you to contact a financial services professional like me to explore how you can leverage life insurance in your financial plan. The purposes I've outlined here may not apply to your situation, but there are several other uses that I haven't mentioned. The bottom line is to have an open mind and be willing to learn beyond the box in which we've historically placed life insurance. Many of these concepts are detailed in my Amazon Best Seller book, *"Increase, Protect, and Dominate Your Money"*, available at TheRealMoneyCoach.com.

About Tony R. Jackson

Tony R. Jackson, "The Real Money Coach," is remarkable and has excelled in multiple domains, including finance, entrepreneurship, and ministry. He has received numerous industry accolades as a highly successful Financial Services Professional. Tony is a 2023 Presidential Lifetime Achievement Award recipient and a certified financial education instructor. Throughout his career, he has held various financial leadership positions. He founded The Real Money Coach, where he empowers individuals through financial literacy and empowerment. Tony's expertise has made him highly sought-after as a presenter and trainer. In addition, he captivates audiences as a frequent guest on Radio One Charlotte, local TV, and a weekly Live show.

Tony resides in Charlotte, North Carolina, and shares a fulfilling life with his beloved wife, Alisa. They have four wonderful children and five awesome grandchildren. Alongside his professional achievements, Tony is also an ordained minister with over 20 years of leadership experience in ministry. His passion for serving others and his faith have been guiding principles. Tony's favorite quote from the movie Black Panther resonates deeply with him: "A man who has not prepared his children for his own death has failed as a father."

NOTES

NOTES

NOTES

NOTES

THE PURPOSE OF OPM "OTHER PEOPLE'S MONEY"

Dr. Rosie Thomas

In the ever-evolving business world, using Other People's Money (OPM) effectively is the real cheat code. OPM refers to leveraging funds from external sources—investors, loans, or partnerships—to fuel your business's growth. It is a strategic move allowing you to grow your business without depleting your resources. While this concept is simple in theory, its application requires strategic planning, a solid business structure, and an understanding of maximizing the benefits while minimizing risks. This chapter delves into the strategic rationale behind leveraging other people's money, what's needed to access OPM, and the benefits and risks involved.

For over twenty years, I have been helping business owners navigate the complexities of financial management. One of the key lessons I emphasize is the importance of understanding and utilizing OPM effectively. It's not just about acquiring capital; it's about making that capital work for you as efficiently and profitably as possible.

Business Structure: Laying the Foundation

Before diving into the world of OPM, your business must be structured properly. Your business structure is the foundation upon which all other aspects of your business rest. Whether you're a sole proprietor, part of a partnership, or an LLC or corporation, the right structure will influence how you manage OPM. Operating as an LLC is the most common structure because it protects your personal assets. Once you determine the right structure for your business, you will register your business by forming a legal entity and obtaining an Employer Identification Number (EIN). An EIN, issued by the IRS, acts as your business's Social Security number and is essential for opening business accounts and applying for credit.

Separate personal from business finances by opening a business bank account to manage your business's financial transactions. This helps establish your business as a separate entity and simplifies record-keeping. Establishing a business address and phone number adds credibility to your business. Use a commercial address rather than a home address, set up a dedicated phone line for your business, and list it in directories.

Bookkeeping: Keeping the Books Balanced

Once your business structure is in place, meticulous bookkeeping becomes the next critical step. When applying for funding, the lenders will request financial statements generated by proper bookkeeping practices. The most common financial statements are profit and loss statements and balance sheets. These financial statements will show the lender was coming in (income) and what's going out (expenses). Proper bookkeeping ensures that your business finances are in order, making it easier to track income, expenses, and, most importantly, the effective use of OPM.

When utilizing OPM, tracking how every dollar is spent is important. This transparency builds trust with investors and ensures you can repay loans or distribute profits as promised. Moreover, accurate bookkeeping is essential for tax preparation and strategizing, which are key components in maximizing the benefits of OPM.

Tax Preparation: Reporting Income and Expenses

Tax preparation is another critical area where businesses can benefit from professional guidance, especially when dealing with OPM. The goal is not just to comply with tax laws but to strategically plan your taxes to report income without writing everything off on your taxes. Lenders often request your tax returns when reporting income to apply for OPM. The net income reported on your tax return is the annual reported income for your business. Most business owners need help with reporting a significant amount of expenses, which reduces their net income. Many tax strategies will cut your tax bill while still reporting income. The two most common strategies used are depreciation and business mileage. While both will reduce your tax bill, lenders still consider the deducted amount of income.

For example, consider a client purchasing a home whose business shows a net income of $750,000 annually based on bank account records. However, the tax return only reflects $350,000 because $400,000 was reported as business expenses. Although the net income is $750,000, the lender will use the income reported on the tax return. On the other hand, if the $400,000 were due to depreciation or business mileage, the net income for lending purposes would be $750,000.

Credit: Personal and Business

Your personal credit can play a significant role when applying for business funding or business credit. Many lenders require a personal guarantee, meaning you're responsible if the business fails to repay the debt. Lenders review your personal credit history to assess your reliability and financial responsibility. It's best to have good to excellent credit (700+), improving your chances of getting business funding. If your personal score is in this range, lenders are more likely to offer favorable terms, such as lower interest rates and higher credit limits.

Register with the business credit bureaus Dun & Bradstreet, Experian, and Equifax to ensure your business is on their radar. Obtain a D-U-N-S Number from Dun & Bradstreet. This is a unique identifier for your business and essential for building your credit profile. Lenders may rely more on your personal credit to gauge risk if your business is new or has a limited credit history. Over time, as your business establishes its credit history, its creditworthiness will become more influential. *Credit Tip: Lenders are likely to approve you for a business credit card or funding if you have a relationship with them and are in good standing.* For example, if you have a personal credit card with an institution or lender, you would likely be approved for a credit card for your business.

Business Funding: Fueling Growth with OPM

One of the primary reasons for spending other people's money is to fuel growth. In the early stages of a business, cash flow is often limited. Entrepreneurs might have a groundbreaking idea or an innovative product but lack the capital required to bring it to market. You can accelerate your business's growth trajectory without waiting to amass personal savings by securing funding from investors, banks, or other sources.

For example, I wanted to create a CRM (customer relationship manager) for business owners to assist with marketing and daily tasks. Developing the CRM required a substantial investment in developing the product, hiring talent, and marketing. With access to funding, I could expedite the development, enter the market sooner, and capture a significant market share before competitors.

Using other people's money can also enhance your financial flexibility. When you can access external funds, you can allocate your resources to other strategic areas. This could include diversifying your investments, setting up emergency reserves, or pursuing new business opportunities. Relationships are key when obtaining business funding and credit. I always suggest starting with your bank when applying for funding because they hold your money and see your cash flow. Small credit unions are also a good source when building relationships. Their interest rates are usually lower; you know your banker and can negotiate terms.

Conclusion: The Power of OPM

Leveraging Other People's Money is more than just a financial strategy; it's a pathway to achieving your business dreams. However, to harness the full power of OPM, it's essential to have a solid foundation—starting with a well-structured business, meticulous bookkeeping, accurate tax returns, good credit, and a clear understanding of your funding options.

With over 20 years of experience, I have seen the transformative power OPM can have on businesses of all sizes. At Thomas Financial, we are committed to guiding our clients through every step of this journey, ensuring they secure the funding they need and use it effectively to build a thriving, successful business. The purpose of OPM is not just to access capital but to create opportunities for growth, innovation, and long-term success. By working with the right partners and implementing sound financial strategies, you can unlock your business's full potential and achieve the success you've always envisioned.

About Dr. Rosie Thomas

Dr. ShaTonya "Rosie" Thomas, known as "The Texas Tax Pro," is a rising star in the Business and Accounting industry and a proud Dallas, Texas native. She founded Thomas Financial in 2009, now a thriving enterprise dedicated to "Wealth Empowerment, We Represent." Her company serves over a thousand clients annually, maximizing tax refunds and savings for individuals and businesses. Her top-selling Tax Pro Planners have also become essential tools for tracking income, expenses, budgets, and mileage.

With her charisma and reach, Dr. Rosie has guided countless business owners in structuring and scaling their finances through her innovative coaching programs. Known for empowering young minority entrepreneurs, she offers customized curricula, business credit services, and tax resources. Dr. Rosie also co-authored Amazon's No. 1 Best Seller, "Tax Strategies for Small Businesses." Her accolades include the Global Humanitarian Award at the Biggest Boss Gala, the Wealth Builder Award at the Family Wealth Builders' Summit, and the Presidential Lifetime Achievement Award from President Biden. She has been featured in Sheen Magazine as a "Woman on the Move," Success Magazine for tax deduction insights, and The Grio for tax-saving strategies. Visit ThomasFinancialLLC.com

NOTES

NOTES

NOTES

NOTES

THE PURPOSE OF TRAINING YOUTH AS HEALERS

Dr. Ruby Mendenhall

The heart of my work centers on creating a new world for our Black and brown youth that allows them to harness their inherent power and leadership to cultivate healing communities. Decades of scholarship show the long-term health consequences of trauma exposure. Several years ago, Lisa Butler and I interviewed the late Dr. Carl Bell for "What's Left Behind?", our documentary about mothers who lost adult children to gun violence. Dr. Bell, an African American professor and founder of a community health organization in Chicago, began a lifelong quest to understand the immediate and long-term consequences of trauma in children in 1976 after working with a young girl who saw her mother shot. Dr. Bell's groundbreaking work was highlighted when scholars conducted the Adverse Childhood Experiences (ACEs) study in a primarily white, middle-aged, college-educated population.

Scholars later expanded the ACE study to include lived experiences of marginalization and oppression. An expanded ACEs study conducted in Philadelphia included new questions about witnessing beatings, stabbings, or shootings, as well as questions about racial and ethnic discrimination, neighborhood safety, being bullied, and foster care experiences. The study showed that those with four or more ACEs had an increased risk of substance abuse, depression, and suicidality. This research highlights the importance of centering our youth's health and wellness and providing them with protective childhood experiences.

Individuals interested in fostering youth's health and wellness must recognize that ACEs are just one side of the coin in child development. The Centers for Disease Control amplifies individual and community protective factors that allow youth to avoid traumatic experiences, heal, and reach their optimal potential. Some of these individual protective factors include a safe and nurturing home environment, positive peer and social networks, doing well in school with support from adults, a caring adult who helps with challenges and provides supervision, having their basic needs met (e.g., food, shelter, and health services), caregivers with college degrees and steady employment, and families experiencing fun activities and joy together. Community protective factors are having access to financial resources, medical care, and mental health services, safe and stable housing, childcare, culturally responsive and engaging schools, after-school programs/activities, quality pre-schools, family-friendly work policies, strong community partnerships, and a felt sense of community and caring.

The Youth Wellness Project and Innovation

The Youth Wellness Project (YWP), co-led by Rachel Switzky and me, fosters individual—and community-level healing and protective factors. Centering Youth's Health and Wellness: Designing a Third Reconstruction and Chicago Renaissance[1] was launched in 2022 with John D. and Catherine T. MacArthur Foundation funding.

A Third Reconstruction

We believe a third reconstruction is required for Black youth to heal and flourish. This includes transforming society to promote a bi-directional exchange of knowledge between universities and communities, new forms of innovation to address entrenched social problems (e.g., poverty and lack of affordable homes), and generating intergenerational wealth via entrepreneurship. YWP has trained 50 youth as Community Health Workers (CHWs) and Citizen/Community Scientists (CSs) to jumpstart the Third Reconstruction. CHWs are trusted individuals, usually from the community they serve, who serve as a bridge to the traditional healthcare system. Citizen/Community Scientists are individuals from the community who work with social, behavioral, and life scientists to produce new knowledge about health, disease, and flourishing that is human-centered, community-based, and interdisciinary. Our CHWs and CSs are helping us to redesign society in a way that allows them to thrive and prosper despite racism and other forms of oppression.

The Youth CHWs and CSs Share Their Lived Experiences

Gun violence has a lot of consequences regarding. Children who may be aware of the situation may have been traumatized. The families [are] affected and need therapy. You limit the freedom of children not being able to go outside and play as a child. It's very limiting, and sadly, I had to grow up that way. (Community Health Worker)

In 1964, Civil Rights leader Fannie Lou recounted her lived experiences about

---

1   Peniel, J.E. 2022. *The Third Reconstruction: America's Struggle for Racial Justice in the Twenty-first Century*. New York. Basic Books. Barber, E.J. 2016. *The Third Reconstruction: How a Moral Movement is Overcoming the Politics of Division and Fear*. Boston: Beacon Press.

the horrors of being Black in America before famously saying, "And I've been tired for so long, now I am sick and tired of being sick and tired." She was referring to what Dr. Arline Geronimus refers to as the "weathering process" that takes place in marginalized individuals' bodies, minds and spirits.[2] Tragically, our youth are also sick and tired of what oppression does to them and their communities. Earlier, I discussed family and community factors that help protect youth against ACEs and their consequences. During a post-training conversation, we asked our CHWs about their lived experiences. One of the CHWs described how the information they learned helped to bring their family members closer together.

My family's notoriously bad at de-stressing, but it's gotten better. I recently started communicating my needs more with my mom. We used to have a rocky relationship. I would get grounded very often, but now that I communicate all my needs and want to hang out with them, even though I'm 17 and a senior, my mom wouldn't expect me to want to hang out with her. Ever since then, it's been a lot less stressful.

This young person, among others, highlighted how Black youth need and want to be loved. We discussed Gary Chapman's five love languages and asked them about their love languages. One Black male said that his love language was reassuring. Shortly after he spoke, another Black male agreed that this was his love language.

New Knowledge and My Mental Shift

It took me a minute to shift away from Chapman's five love languages that I knew and to try to understand what these young Black males were telling us. Their words illuminated the need for a paradigm shift in thinking about the love that Black youth need. What types of reassurance do they need from us? Did their need for love as reassurance signify that they have been injured and feel in danger? Is this their request for reassurance, a way to cope with the heavy burdens of oppression and weathering? Do they need us to see beyond their aggressive or stoic behaviors and light up when they enter our presence?

---

2   Geronimus, A.T. 2023. *Weathering: The Extraordinary Stress of Ordinary Life in an Unjust Society.* New York: Little, Brown Spark.

I received another glimpse into this need for reassurance as the youth talked about how many friends and relatives they lost to gun violence. I was emotionally shaken (meaning I cried on the inside) as I listened to them tell their stories. I was also angry and hopeless because the problem seemed significant and devastating. After the session ended, I called the therapist who was available to the young people and their families and asked if she could spend some time with the young people (and me) talking about grief and coping, including cultivating hope. We believe hope is a crucial aspect of dealing with adversity in life. We then launched the Youth DREAM Incubator™, which inspires young people to imagine and create a just world (Third Reconstruction) through innovation, inventions, and entrepreneurship.

We Are Not Without Hope

Ruby Mendenhall, 2024 Urbana IL Poet Laureate

We are not without hope

We hear the whispers

Of our ancestors

Saying to us

Don't back down

Our humanity knows no bounds

The youth are the bridge to tomorrow

Let them stand with you

And then on their own

They are prepared for a world

That you will never know

Give them roots and wings

So, they can be powerful

Beyond our imaginations

About Dr. Ruby Mendenhall

Dr. Ruby Mendenhall was born in Chicago, IL. Both parents migrated from the South. After graduating high school, she wanted to be a poet but needed to learn to become one professionally. Therefore, she continued to write many poems, pursued a bachelor's degree in Occupational Therapy, and worked at the Cook County (now John Stroger Hospital of Cook County) in Chicago. Her dreams were realized when she became the 2024 City of Urbana's Poet Laureate. Mendenhall also has a master's degree in Public Policy and a Ph.D. in Human Development and Social Policy.

Dr. Mendenhall is the Kathryn Lee Baynes Dallenbach LAS Professor in Sociology and African American Studies at the University of Illinois at Urbana-Champaign. She is an associate dean at the Carle Illinois College of Medicine and an associate director of the Cancer Center in Illinois. Mendenhall's research examines how living in racially segregated neighborhoods with high levels of violence affects Black mothers' mental and physical health using surveys, interviews, crime statistics, police records, data from 911 calls, art, wearable sensors, and genomic analysis. She co-directs the Youth Wellness Project, which trains youth as Community Health Workers and Citizen/Community Scientists and creates Wellness Stores/Spaces. For more information, visit https://igpa.uillinois.edu/tag/ruby-mendenhall.

NOTES

NOTES

NOTES

NOTES

THE PURPOSE OF INTENTIONALITY

Bria Grant

From Rural Roots to Urban Heights: My Journey

Introduction

My life has been shaped by resilience, determination, and an unwavering commitment to service. Born in rural Mississippi and later raised in the urban landscape of Milwaukee, Wisconsin, I've had my fair share of challenges and triumphs. My story is one of turning adversity into opportunity, from experiencing childhood abandonment to becoming a mother of two and navigating the complexities of marriage and divorce. Through it all, I've remained focused on my purpose, driven by the belief that intentionality can lead to transformative change.

Early Life

From rural Mississippi to urban Milwaukee, I was born in a small town where life was simple, and community bonds were strong. My earliest memories are of wide-open fields and the quiet rhythms of country life. But even in this seemingly idyllic setting, I faced a significant challenge—being abandoned at a young age. This experience could have broken me, but it became my resilience's foundation. I learned early on that I had to rely on myself and that strength would carry me through many of life's challenges. When I moved to Milwaukee, everything changed. The city was a stark contrast to the rural environment I had known. It was vibrant, fast-paced, and, at times, overwhelming. But it was also in Milwaukee that I began to understand the disparities within communities—disparities that fueled my desire to make a difference. The challenges I saw around me, particularly in health and social justice, sparked a fire in me that would guide my future endeavors.

Education

Education was my escape, empowering myself to create the change I wanted to see in the world. I pursued a Bachelor's degree in Human Services at Springfield College School of Human Services, and in May 2007, I graduated with a deep understanding of the social systems that shape our lives. This wasn't just an academic achievement for me—it was a stepping stone to something greater, a way to equip myself with the tools needed to address the inequities I had witnessed. But my journey of learning didn't stop there. In August 2010, I completed a Certification of Completion from the Center for Progressive Leadership (CPL). I honed my leadership skills and deepened my understanding of the political and social landscapes that impact our communities. This experience prepared me for my challenges as a leader and change-maker.

In 2017, I expanded my knowledge by obtaining a certification of completion from the Association for Commercial Real Estate (ACRE). This was a significant step for me, as it allowed me to explore the intersection of community development and economic empowerment—particularly in underserved areas. I wanted to understand how real estate could be a tool for lifting communities, not just a means of personal gain. I'm pursuing a Master's in Public Health at the Medical College of Wisconsin. This is a natural progression in my journey, aligning perfectly with my mission to address public health challenges at both the local and national levels. I've always believed that education is a lifelong journey, and I'm committed to continuously growing and learning to make a meaningful impact.

Personal Life

Marriage, motherhood, divorce, and my personal life have been as rich and complex as my professional journey. I experienced the highs and lows of marriage, a relationship that brought its own set of challenges. Ultimately, my marriage ended in divorce—a difficult but necessary decision that reflected my commitment to prioritizing my well-being and that of my children. Motherhood has been one of the most profound experiences of my life. As a mother of two, I've had to balance the demands of my career with the responsibilities of raising my children. It hasn't always been easy, but it has been gratifying. My children are my greatest joy; they have given me a deeper understanding of many families' struggles. This, in turn, has fueled my commitment to my work in community health and public service.

Professional Beginnings

Laying the foundation for my professional journey began with challenging but deeply impactful roles. One of my earliest positions was as an AODA (Alcohol and Other Drug Abuse) Counselor at ATTIC Correctional Services, where I worked from September 2010 to August 2012. In this role, I had the opportunity to help individuals who were often at the margins of society, grappling with substance abuse and the difficulties of reintegration. Working as the Lead Substance Abuse Counselor and Primary and Aftercare Drug Treatment Program Coordinator, I was able to make a significant impact on the lives of those who often felt lost and alone. This experience was eye-opening—it solidified my understanding of the complex relationship between social determinants of health and individual well-being. It also reinforced my belief that real change required a broader, community-wide approach.

Ascending Leadership

My vision emerged as I took on more substantial roles in my career, and my leadership potential became increasingly evident. From December 2013, I served as the Operations Director for the Milwaukee Area Health Education Center (MAHEC). MAHEC's mission—improving the health of underserved communities through collaborative partnerships—deeply resonated with my values and aspirations. I enhanced the organization's operational processes and policies in this role, ensuring that MAHEC could effectively fulfill its mission. I was responsible for managing and increasing the efficiency of support services, including human resources, information technology, and finance. My contributions improved MAHEC's internal operations and strengthened its ability to serve the community. I was also actively involved in long-term planning initiatives to achieve operational excellence. My ability to analyze best practices and evaluate evidence-based research in healthcare-focused career development demonstrated my dedication to continuous improvement and commitment to creating lasting change.

Founding UniteWI: A Vision of Transformative Impact

In November 2016, I took a leap of faith and founded UniteWI, a national Pathways Community HUB based in Milwaukee. UniteWI was born from my deep commitment to addressing social and health disparities in my community and beyond.

The organization's mission is to improve social and health outcomes by reducing social risks and ensuring that care coordination services are available to meet the population's needs. As the Executive Director of UniteWI, I've been at the forefront of efforts to expand and extend the organization's reach to communities throughout

Wisconsin. My leadership has been instrumental in establishing policies and programs that address health disparities, particularly in underserved areas. Under my guidance, UniteWI has developed a robust referral network and contracted with various payers to fund the organization's services. These efforts have significantly improved access to care and support for those in need.

My role at UniteWI is multifaceted, encompassing everything from strategic planning to day-to-day operations. I work closely with the Board of Directors and various committees to ensure our programs align with our mission.

Developing and maintaining relationships with other agencies and organizations has been critical to our success, and I take pride in the collaborative spirit that drives our work. One of the core principles of my leadership is a focus on data management and evidence-based practices. I understand that to address health disparities effectively, we must have accurate and reliable data. This approach has allowed us to identify areas of need and allocate resources more effectively, ensuring that we make the greatest impact possible.

In addition to my work at UniteWI, I've continued contributing to the community through my consulting business, BGrant Consulting LLC, which I founded in October 2009. I've provided many professional services through this business, including project management, public affairs, government relations, civic engagement, and marketing research. My clients have included local community organizations, Milwaukee Public Schools, and various health promotion programs.

Community Engagement and Leadership

My commitment to the community extends beyond my professional roles. I've been actively involved in various boards and organizations, using my expertise to influence positive change.

As a member of the Governor's Milwaukee Child Welfare Partnership Council and the City of Milwaukee Health Department Board of Health, I've played a crucial role in shaping policies that impact the well-being of Milwaukee's residents. My leadership extends to the Milwaukee Crime Stoppers Board and the African American Ladies Empowering Growth and Opportunity (A-LEGO) organization, where I serve as the

Health/Mental Health Chair. These roles reflect my deep commitment to addressing health, safety, and empowerment issues within the African American community.

My involvement in international organizations, such as WILL/WAND, demonstrates my broader commitment to women's leadership and empowerment. As a founding board member of Janus College Preparatory and Arts Academy, I've also contributed to the education and development of future generations.

Conclusion

My life has been shaped by a deep sense of purpose and a commitment to intentionality. From my rural beginnings in Mississippi to my role as a leader in Milwaukee, I've always been driven by a desire to improve the lives of others. Despite the challenges I've faced—childhood abandonment, navigating marriage and divorce, and raising two children—I've remained focused on my mission to create positive change. Through my work at UniteWI, consulting business, and involvement in various community initiatives, I'm committed to paving the way for a healthier, more equitable future for all. My journey is far from over, and I'm excited to see where my path of intentionality will lead next.

As the Executive Director of UNITEWI, I am passionate about improving the health outcomes of populations through addressing social determinants of health and strengthening the workforce of Community Health Workers (CHWs). With a Bachelor's degree in Human Services from Springfield College and over 20 years of experience in business consulting, community development, strategic planning, and workforce development, I have developed and implemented strategies that promote health equity and social justice in Wisconsin and beyond.

In collaboration with government agencies, healthcare providers, community organizations, and non-governmental organizations, I have secured nearly $30 million in funding to support various initiatives that leverage the role of CHWs in improving health and preventing disease. Some of the notable achievements include securing the first-ever Wisconsin Medicaid HMO contract that reimburses social determinants of health using CHWs, expanding the CHW workforce across Wisconsin, developing the "Wisconsin Healthy Hearts Protocol" and developing the first WI Department of Workforce Development CHW apprenticeship program. I also serve on several boards and affiliations that align with my vision and values, such as the Wisconsin Community Health Worker Network, the City of Milwaukee Board of Health, and the Wisconsin Black Child Development Institute.

About Bria Grant

Bria Grant serves as the Executive Director of UNITEWI, where she is deeply committed to enhancing health outcomes by addressing social determinants of health and strengthening the workforce of Community Health Workers (CHWs). She holds a Bachelor's in Human Services from Springfield College and has over 20 years of experience in business consulting, community development, strategic planning, and workforce development. She has implemented strategies promoting health equity and social justice in Wisconsin and beyond throughout her career.

Grant has successfully collaborated with government agencies, healthcare providers, community organizations, and NGOs to secure nearly $30 million in funding. These funds have supported initiatives that leverage CHWs in health improvement and disease prevention, including securing Wisconsin's first Medicaid HMO contract reimbursing social determinants of health through CHWs, expanding the CHW workforce statewide, creating the "Wisconsin Healthy Hearts Protocol," and developing the state's first CHW apprenticeship program with the Department of Workforce Development. She also serves on several boards that align with her vision, including the Wisconsin Community Health Worker Network, the City of Milwaukee Board of Health, and the Wisconsin Black Child Development Institute.

NOTES

NOTES

NOTES

THE PURPOSE OF EXCEEDING URBAN CULTURAL STEREOTYPES AND IDEOLOGIES

Fredrick "Bugzy" Taylor

Urban culture is "the presence of a large population in a limited space following social norms." These social norms are, in turn, influenced by the social interactions and ideologies constructed within that milieu. Furthermore, urban culture is synonymous with black struggle, perseverance, and the ability to exist and create within those conditions. But sadly, in our culture, one of the most common mistakes is believing that our environment constrains us in terms of our habits, behaviors, and accomplishments. This is a fundamental error used by others to disenfranchise black culture from capital success. Still, we also must bear some responsibility for limiting the ideas of what success looks and means for us. Regrettably, we live in a day and time where it's far too common to express indifference when achievements, goals, and lifestyles differ from our socio-economic norms. *This*, too, is an error that needs immediate correction!

Not only are today's urban cultural stereotypes harmful to adopt, they are synonymous with the civil rights era when black men and women were reduced to roles and expectations that were unparalleled to white Americans. Those stereotypes and ideologies are the same today because they are founded upon the proverbial anchor of subjective limitations. Think back to the times when women were subjugated to roles lesser than their counterparts. Think back to when African American women were reduced to roles more inferior than African American men. Men, who were at that time, deemed unequal to white men in every aspect! This brings to mind the challenges that great women such as Shirley Chisholm faced.

Shirley Chisholm was born during a time coined by historians as America's "Great Depression." This event occurred in 1929 when the United States stock market crashed. Worldwide, America and its economy were viewed as politically unstable and in dire financial decline. What isn't widely known is that the "Great Migration" (1919-1970) took place before and after "The Great Depression." It was an era when African American men and women fled the North, physically and mentally, escaping the Jim Crow South along with its prejudices and racist laws that bound them to limited freedoms and unjust treatment. Consequently, the "New Negro Movement" began in the 1920s and was fueled by the arts, culture, and intellectuals to publicize racial pride, self-expression, and social reform within politics. During America's time of plight and decline, African Americans were advocating and demanding their release from societal designations, expectations, and the injustices America imposed on them.

As a young girl, Shirley Chisholm must have embodied the spirit and energies circulating then. She would excel, assume the position of an American politician, and later earn the Presidential Medal of Freedom. Not only was she (as a black woman) viewed by white Americans with limited scope, but she was likely viewed that way by the majority of the black men she encountered every day. For this reason, she would later be quoted as saying, *"We must not only reject the stereotypes that others have of us but also that we have of ourselves."* She knew the detriment of accepting and embodying the stereotypes and expectations others projected onto her. Because of her insight and refusal to fall within labels and perceptual confinements, Shirley Chisholm would later become the first black woman elected to the United States Congress. She courageously represented New York's congressional district for seven terms and later became the first black nomination for President of the United States.

When America saw itself in a period of plight and depression, black people (the inventors of urban culture) had every odd against them. Yet, they sought higher grounds and demands. They refused to be confined by ideologies and stereotypes. But somehow, in the new Millennium, we still struggle with those same racial biases projected and imposed upon us, just as it was with our ancestors during and post-slavery. Today, we struggle because America has permeated the country with adverse generalizations and ideas that blatantly degrade black men and women. Every form of media (radio, TV, social, and print) pushes the misperception of what it means to be a black man or woman—angry, drug addict, lazy, money-hungry, sexual deviant, thuggery, uneducated, and violent.

These images and messages to African American youth and young adults lack depth or value and minimize the importance of being both responsible and accountable adults. Additionally, it falsely promotes the idea that African Americans have some unequivocal measurement of success and attainment in comparison to White Americans. We can see this exemplified throughout black urban culture, and unfortunately, this generation, more than any other, has naively welcomed the Trojan horse with open arms. These designations are no longer damaging to us and are almost always grossly overlooked. We willfully segregate ourselves regarding residential and commercial ownership, political education, involvement, and unconventional business endeavors. Presently, we are neither prominent in these areas nor do we prioritize excelling in them because we view them as culturally opposing.

Urban culture has perverted and misconstrued the idea of what it means to be "Gangsta," a "Hood Nigga," or a "Real Nigga." Whether conscious or through ignorance, we have now created a false persona that excludes growth and development beyond urban scope and image. Terms such as "sellout," "crossover," and "mainstream" are used when black men and women seek a vaster role in business and lifestyle uncommon to urban culture. I hate to say this, but white men and women who have that "Old South" mentality *prey* on our literal and conceptual marginality. They accomplish such oppressive tactics by using the proverbial "fence" to keep us within limits and out of larger, more diversified business ventures. Today, they prey on our lack of awareness and use acculturative business tactics to tap into our community and siphon our money to widen the cultural gap further. They do this *successfully* by highlighting cultural ideologies that lead us to believe certain habits, behaviors, and lifestyles are stereotypically more befitting of us. This, of course, could be an arguable assumption if not for the fact that America is one big gumbo pot! A country of immense diversity in race and religion with a promise to all to have the right to pursue happiness—*however* that joy may be.

Like Master P said years ago, there *"Ain't no limit!"* What is for us isn't confined by a genre or in a box. Think about it! We were not meant to traverse the roads of slavery, prejudice, and diversity to be given a "certain type of lifestyle!" How fortunate would America be if it were not a country where we can *all* acquire, explore, own, and enjoy what it offers? Not fortunate at all! That is why we should be intentional in our efforts to exceed urban cultural stereotypes. We not only owe it to civil rights leaders and activists who fought and became the catalysts of change and reform. We owe it to ourselves! This debt is due to us every time one of those "Old-South-minded" individuals looks at us and labels us anything but an equal opportunity man or woman.

Our socioeconomic status does not determine the definition of who we are. So, when asked, "What is the purpose of exceeding urban cultural stereotypes?" Our response should be: "My purpose derives from the lives lost and battles fought by men and women incapable of seeking opportunities and acquiring the wealth and luxuries we are now promised. My purpose rests on the souls of the slaughtered and enslaved, the hearts and heads of the men and women who were victims of injustice and incarceration—the children victimized by redline housing and poor education— the homes broken by addiction due to the intentional influx of drugs and guns. Exceeding stereotypical limits imposed on people like me enables me to tear down those boundaries that obstruct me from reaching true mastery of wealth. Wealth in the form and fashion my ancestors and leaders envisioned for me!"

About Fredrick "Bugzy" Taylor

Fredrick "Bugzy" Taylor is an author, Drug and Alcohol Counselor, and passionate advocate for social and restorative justice. With over 35 years of experience in Ohio's foster homes, group homes, juvenile detention centers, and the nation's state and federal prison systems, he has gained a profound understanding of the challenges faced by those in similar life circumstances. Taylor's extensive background enables him to connect with individuals dealing with comparable hardships, offering them guidance and support.

Taylor firmly believes that America has long addressed its community challenges through a punitive lens. In response, he now uses his experiences to provide youth with guidance, deterrence, direction, and mentorship for individuals and families affected by incarceration. His book, *How to Beat the System*, offers readers practical strategies for managing, coping with, and overcoming adversity. His mission is to inspire, enlighten, and restore the mental and physical well-being of individuals living in America's marginalized communities.

NOTES

NOTES

NOTES

THE TRANSFORMATIONAL PURPOSE OF OUR WORDS

"In the beginning was the Word, and the Word was with God, and the Word was God." John 1:1

Dr. Joel "JP" Martin

Many people use the word "Transformation," so much so that it has become common. Transformation is not a cliche but a profound journey of change and growth. It implies a deep, fundamental shift beyond surface-level changes or minor adjustments. It is about altering the essence of something, whether that is an individual's mindset, an organization's culture, or a society's way of thinking.

Our ability to make and keep commitments to ourselves and others gives us an awareness of self-control and the courage and strength to accept the responsibility of our lives. Our honor overrides our moods. "If it's to be, it's up to me" is more than a slogan; it is an affirmation that is lived.

Transformation involves looking at oneself and the world in a new way. With purposeful words, we create our vision without the permission or authority of others or any evidence or certainty that what we say will happen. Are there circumstances? Yes, but we are senior to the circumstances, which means we have them; they do not have us. We are authentic and exhibit the quality of being honest, genuine, truthful, trustworthy, and a people of our word. Being actually and precisely what we claim to be. This requires that our behaviors prove what we claim and honor ourselves and others as our word in action.

The transformational power of our words lies in their ability to bring new realities into existence or catalyze events that otherwise might not have happened. Every word we speak, consciously or unconsciously, shapes outcomes that align with its intent. Words possess the power to make or break, to inspire or discourage, to heal or harm. A single, purposeful word can plant the seeds of change, spark a movement, or give life to a vision. For example, Rev. Dr. Martin Luther King Jr.'s historic "I Have a Dream" speech didn't just convey hope; it fueled an enduring movement for justice, equality, and transformation. In this way, intentional words carry the potential to reshape the world around us.

If your goal is to elevate your business, secure sponsorships, shift to a new career, establish multiple income streams while relaxing on the beach, or become an international speaker and trainer—whatever your highest aspirations—the Bible captures this power of intention in Proverbs 18:21: "The tongue has the power of life and death, and those who love it will eat its fruit" (NIV). A powerful strategy for achieving your desired success is "Be–Do–Have."

Consider the qualities of a child—curiosity, adventure, and an open heart. Reflect on how you were as a child and the lessons you gathered as you grew. Now, envision the compelling future that beckons you. Imagine yourself fully embodying the visionary person you aspire to be. "Act as though." Be that person now. Speak it into existence now: make your "I am" declaration: I am a ____ (adjective), _____ (adjective) (noun).

First, Be the person you envision, then Do what it takes to Have what you genuinely want to create. Is your goal to become the business leader transforming a struggling company into an industry giant? Or the visionary whose words ignite a global movement? You aspire to be the coach who empowers clients to break through their limits with inspiring language or the consultant whose insights lead organizations to unprecedented success. Whatever it is—go for it!

There's a common expression, "If I see it, I'll believe it," but it's more accurate to say, "If I believe it, I'll see it." The following strategy offers a way to unlock freedom through the power of words. Here's a model for understanding this:

Event → Belief → Emotion → Behavior (what you say and do) **→ Consequences** (internal results from your behavior: positive consequences reinforce your actions, while negative ones can stop or redirect them based on your response) **→ Impact** (the effect of your behavior on others).

Have To—Choose To: Ever feel weighed down by things you "have to" do? This exercise helps challenge the beliefs behind those feelings. For this experiment, define a "Have To" as something you feel obligated to do or be—even though you usually don't enjoy it. Make a list of these "Have To" items. Then, say each one aloud with conviction: "I have to ____." Repeat each for about 2 minutes. Did you feel displeasure, anger, sadness, or a sense of being burdened or trapped?

Say that same list, but start each item with "I get to" or "I choose to" for about 2 minutes. How did that feel? Did you experience pleasure, joy, or release—a feeling of freedom and choice? That's the power of intentional language; it gives you agency.

The difference between a "Have To" and a "Choose To" is your mindset. As the saying goes, "You can't get the latitude if you don't have the attitude."

Beliefs remain fixed until we challenge, face, and choose to change them. No one can make us shift our beliefs—we must be willing to do this on our own or with the help of an experienced coach. Influential and successful people consistently do this.

Additional strategies to elevate your journey: By intentionally choosing our words, we can rewrite our stories and shape our futures. Tools like affirmations, declarations, and sincere acknowledgments help dismantle limiting beliefs and create new possibilities. Dedicate a few minutes each morning to writing or speaking positive affirmations, and start your day with a prayer. Focus on the areas where you want to grow and improve. Monitor your self-talk throughout the day, replacing negative statements with positive affirmations. Keep a Gratitude Journal. Engage Accountability Partners and Coaches. And always extend grace to yourself and others.

Big promises come with significant risks that often push us beyond our comfort zones. Sharing your declarations and commitments with accountability partners, such as coaches, coworkers, or family members, can provide the support and encouragement needed to persevere. When promises are kept, take time to acknowledge and celebrate these achievements. Reflect on what worked well and identify areas for improvement. When promises aren't fulfilled, treat it as a growth opportunity. Ask yourself, "What did I learn from this experience that I can apply in the future?" Embracing successes and challenges allows you to refine your approach and move closer to your goals continually. Sharing your promises with others fosters accountability and serves as a powerful motivator.

Each of us was put on this earth with a unique purpose. Your journey to mastering wealth with your words continues. Embrace the challenge, experiment with new language patterns, and observe their transformative impact on your life. Every word you speak is a seed planted in the garden of your reality. Cultivate these words with care, and watch your world bloom.

As the Ibo proverb says, "It is not what you call me but what I answer to." This speaks to our ability to define our self-worth. Ultimately, it's how you see yourself and what you respond to that truly matters, not the opinions or labels others might give. We can see ourselves as the creators of our destiny, emotions, and attitudes. This perspective may not be an absolute truth, but it is a powerful stance. As mentioned before, a belief is simply something we accept as true and act upon as if it were fact—your choice.

We will always have our past. Now what? It's not erased. But if we continue to choose actions based on our history, we will create more of the same. Each of us has the power to reinterpret our past, creating a new, empowering narrative. Through intentional, purposeful words, we can speak about our history in a way that serves us. Now, who do you choose to be? What new life are you committed to creating for yourself? Say it loud, and say it with pride.

About Dr. Joel "JP" Martin

Dr. Joel "JP" Martin is President of Triad West Inc. and Founder of the Positively Powerful Education Summit and Woman Awards, is an author, training designer, facilitator, and executive coach with over 20 years of experience as a Transformational Leadership and Diversity, Equity, and Inclusion specialist.

Dr. Martin's commitment to developing successful leaders, aligned teams, and empowered women executives has led her to engagements before Fortune 500 corporations, educational institutions, and business owners in 13 countries and across the US.

She has earned a Ph.D. in Communications and a Master's in Psychology, admission as a Wharton Fellow of Wharton Business School, and membership on the Forbes Coaching Council. She is a member of the African American Women's Giving and Empowerment Circle and launched the 501c3 Positively Powerful Business and Community Development Organization (PPBCD) in January 2024.

Dr. Martin, a recognized figure in her field, has appeared on the Today Show, ABC's Sonoran Living, the NY Times, Black Enterprise, Essence (cover and feature), and Fortune. Previously, she owned and operated a full-service advertising agency specializing in multicultural communications.

A native New Yorker, she now lives in Scottsdale, AZ, with her husband, Bob, a fine artist and oil painter from the Bronx, New York. Visit PositivelyPowerful.com/Insights/

NOTES

NOTES

NOTES

THE PURPOSE OF WEALTH

Dr. Franklin J. Marshall

The Purpose of Wealth can mean different things to different people, but for me, wealth is all about having choices and the ability to do the things you desire. Wealth isn't just about accumulating money or assets; it's about creating a foundation for freedom and flexibility. When you have wealth, you gain the power to design your lifestyle, pursue passions, and focus on what's most important to you. Beyond personal benefit, wealth can be a tool for making a positive impact—whether supporting causes close to your heart, helping others achieve their goals, or contributing to the community meaningfully. Ultimately, wealth offers the opportunity to live fully, purposefully, and with the capacity to leave a lasting legacy.

I live in Powder Springs, Georgia, which holds memories of struggle and triumph. Growing up, I faced numerous obstacles, from financial hardships to the decision to leave school in the 12th grade. Life was challenging, but these experiences taught me resilience, grit, and the value of hard work. Each hardship became a lesson, shaping me into who I am today and inspiring my commitment to growth and success.

Today, I have wealth, which has allowed me to give back to the community that raised me. It's important to me to support my family and the children in inner-city areas who face challenges similar to those I grew up with. When I was young, I promised never to look down on anyone unless I was complimenting their shoes—a reminder to stay humble and kind.

My family taught me the value of learning and building wealth, emphasizing that wealth is not merely about having money but about having choices. With it, I can help those in need, support my community, assist church members, and extend a hand to others in Powder Springs.

I give back through my nonprofit organization, Force of 1, where I teach financial literacy to young men. I work with them weekly on essential financial skills—personal financial management, budgeting, and investing. This knowledge equips them to build a stronger future, using the power of wealth to transform their lives.

Growing up in Powder Springs, I saw many people struggle, and I vowed to make a difference. Wealth has enabled me to do just that. I can now provide resources and support to children in challenging circumstances, helping create a brighter future for them. By teaching financial literacy, I empower others to make wise financial decisions, benefiting their lives and strengthening our community. This is the true purpose of wealth.

When I teach financial literacy, I focus on the basics: understanding income and expenses, creating a budget, saving money, and investing for the future. These are essential skills that everyone needs to know, but they should be taught in schools. By providing this education, I'm helping young men build a solid financial foundation to benefit them for the rest of their lives.

One of the most rewarding aspects of teaching financial literacy is seeing its transformative impact on the young men I work with. Many come from challenging backgrounds, and learning about money management gives them hope for a better future. They start to see that they can take control of their finances and make choices that will improve their lives.

My late wife, Alice, inspired a big part of this journey. She believed sincerely in giving back and supporting others, and her memory continues to guide me. Alice was a kind and loving person who always put others first. Together, we dreamed of creating a better future for our family and community. Although she is no longer with us, her spirit lives on in my work. I honor Alice's memory by continuing the work we started together. She was passionate about helping others, and I strive to carry her legacy through my nonprofit organization. Teaching financial literacy to young men is one way I can make a difference, just as Alice always encouraged me to do.

Alice taught me the value of kindness and looking out for others. She had a way of making everyone feel unique and valued. I bring that same sense of compassion and empathy to my work. Whether teaching a financial literacy class or helping someone in the community, I always remember Alice's example.

Beyond this work, wealth has also allowed me to support my family in ways I never thought possible. I can provide them with a comfortable home, a good education, and opportunities I didn't have growing up. Being a father is one of the most important and rewarding roles in my life, and my children inspire me every day to be the best version of myself. They remind me of the importance of hard work, perseverance, and kindness, and I strive to create a world where they have the opportunities and support they need to succeed.

Wealth has enabled me to live out the values Alice and I shared. It's given me the ability to support my family and help others meaningfully. By teaching financial literacy and giving back to my community, I honor Alice's memory and positively impact the world.

The purpose of wealth extends beyond simply acquiring money; it's about creating choices and having the ability to make a meaningful impact in the lives of others. True wealth enables us to lift those around us, support our loved ones, and invest in a better future for our communities. For me, wealth has been the foundation that allows me to provide security and opportunities for my family and give back in ways that have lasting value.

When used with intention, wealth is a powerful tool for creating a ripple effect of good. It can transform lives, strengthen communities, and lay the groundwork for a better tomorrow. To me, this is the true purpose of wealth—to use it wisely, uplift others, and contribute to a world where everyone can thrive.

Being a father and cherishing the memory of my late wife, Alice, has been the anchor of my journey, providing me with the strength, resilience, and motivation to keep moving forward. Fatherhood has shown me the importance of building a legacy of integrity and kindness. At the same time, Alice's memory reminds me daily of our shared values—compassion, generosity, and an unwavering commitment to uplifting others. These influences are the foundation of my purpose.

I'm also deeply grateful for my team's unwavering support and guidance, whose loyalty and friendship have shaped me into who I am today. Men like Reverend Tracy Carter, Fredrick Jones II, Sidney Montgomery II, and Rodrick Ford have stood by me, each bringing unique wisdom, strength, and dedication. Their influence is felt in every decision I make and every step I take, and I am inspired by the impact we've created together.

Wealth has allowed me to honor their legacies by making a tangible difference in the lives of others. Through this journey, I've understood that true wealth is not just about personal gain but about creating opportunities for those who walk alongside us and those who come after us. This, to me, is the true purpose of wealth: to empower, uplift, and leave a lasting legacy that reflects the values of those we hold dear.

About Dr. Franklin J. Marshal

Dr. Franklin J. Marshall, born on August 26, 1953, in rural Powder Springs, grew up in a single-parent home led by his mother, Naomi Marshals, and his nine siblings. Determined to succeed, he left school in the 12th grade and married Alice, his lifelong partner, with whom he had three children.

Franklin worked diligently as a maintenance man in manufacturing before realizing his dream in 1999 by founding Uncle Frank Maintenance and Cleaning. Through hard work, he built a successful business. After the passing of his beloved wife Alice, with whom he shared 44 years, Franklin felt called to give back to his community. In 2009, he launched Force of 1, a nonprofit focused on helping young people in underserved areas.

Guided by his motto, "I promised the Lord if I ever made it big, I would never look down on anyone unless I was complimenting their shoes," Franklin continues to impact lives. Now a grandfather to nine and a great-grandfather, he remains committed to changing the world, one child at a time.

NOTES

NOTES

NOTES

THE PURPOSE OF PRESERVING HISTORY AND LEGACY THROUGH ART

Ardena L. Brooks

Have you ever wanted to learn more about your ancestors or wondered what achievements your children might pass down to future generations? And what about your own legacy? What enduring mark will you leave for those who come after you? These reflections may help uncover the hidden legacy of your family and highlight the importance of preserving and sharing those stories.

Early Life

My story began in the late 1950s when my dad prepared us for our first family photo. He had recently received a military assignment to the Philippines, which meant that my mom, brother Jerry, and I would not see our grandparents and great-grandmother Julia for the next two years.

As the photographer checked his equipment, my dad seated us in the middle of my grandmother's "do not enter" living room. We were four generations living together in a large, three-story red brick house in northwest Washington, D.C. I was only six, but I still remember the thrill and anticipation of moving to another country. Although finding new friends felt a bit daunting, I knew it would be an unforgettable experience. At the time, though, I didn't understand why that family photo was so significant.

As our family traveled, I took up softball, basketball, volleyball, track, and singing, though art was my true passion. My first major community art project was a historical mural, painted alongside about 20 other artists before the White House in Lafayette Park.

During my senior year in Germany, I continued to pursue art, participating in several projects and winning third place for an abstract oil painting I still have. I owe much of my growth to my Aunt Lois, an artist who took me under her wing and taught me how to refine my skills and boost my confidence.

A Different Direction

Being an artist in the 70s wasn't a typical career path, especially for African Americans, so I began taking business courses in college, working side jobs, and singing in nightclubs. Pursuing college and securing a stable job was generally the expectation.

Eventually, I moved to California with my rock-funk band, Dragon Fly, hoping to land a record deal in Hollywood. What a journey that was! One of my most memorable moments with the band before leaving D.C. was opening for Richard Pryor and Earth, Wind & Fire at the Richmond Coliseum in Virginia. However, breaking into the music industry took a lot of work, especially with limited funds. When Dragon Fly accepted a tour in Japan, I chose a different path: settling down, getting a stable job, and creating a secure home for my daughter. Soon after, I married the band's bass player, Eugene "Bunny" Brooks.

The Purpose

After graduating from the Art Institute of Los Angeles, my life changed. Freelancing became my entrepreneurial focus, and soon after, I was hired as the lead graphic designer at Crenshaw Christian Center. I spent eleven years in the marketing department, primarily working on the ministry's television projects.

I'm grateful for the opportunity to serve as an artist there, as it allowed me to develop my skills further while managing my home-based business, *Designs by Ardena*. One of my most memorable moments at Crenshaw Christian Center was when Dr. Frederick K.C. Price (later known as Apostle Price) called me into his office to thank me for creating a photographic collage highlighting the milestones and legacy of his ministry. Although Apostle Price passed away in February 2021, Crenshaw Christian Center continues to thrive as a beautiful oasis in South Los Angeles, now pastored by his son, Frederick K. Price Jr.

Shortly after, my 99-year-old grandmother passed away just weeks before her hundredth birthday. My brother and I were disappointed she didn't reach that milestone, but what a legacy she left behind. The highlight was discovering that the old family photo among her belongings was still in its original frame. We also found pictures of our great-uncle, Phillip George Barnes, Grandma's brother-in-law, one of the Golden Thirteen—the first African Americans commissioned as Navy officers in 1944.

Like many families, our history is rich with untold stories, so I decided to continue sharing these stories with our children, grandchildren, and great-grandchildren through art. I thank God my grandmother preserved these photos and that my dad insisted on capturing our family's history in that photo, which has now become one of my signature legacy art pieces.

I believe virtually everyone has hidden treasures in their legacy—filled with stories waiting to be preserved and shared with future generations.

So, why are photographs so important? Here are a few reasons:

- Photos capture moments that allow us to recall special memories of family, people, places, and events.

- They serve as visual records of family lineage, tradition, culture, and heritage, preserving genealogical information for generations.

- Photos are frozen snapshots of moments we can never otherwise reclaim, serving as powerful tools for storytelling and sharing experiences.

But what's the purpose? Why preserve these legacy moments through art captured in photos? Using the acronym **ARTS**, I'd like to introduce our signature process for bringing photographs to life through art.

- **A (Assess):** We begin by assessing the photograph's condition to determine if it's a good candidate for repair and restoration as art, ensuring its quality will endure over time.

- **R (Repair):** We repair photos that have faded or suffered damage, including spills, spots, cracks, tears, broken glass, discoloration, missing sections, and fire or water damage. Restoration aims to bring the photo as close to its original clarity as possible.

- **T (Transformation):** Transforming photos into art involves enhancing color, contrast, and vibrancy, giving each piece a fresh, new finish.

- **S (Story):** Everyone has stories. What are yours? We encourage you to uncover and celebrate the stories of your family or business, capturing special moments that will carry forward history and legacy—because your stories matter!

Testimonies

Toney Massey's photo was faded, discolored, and dark. When the artwork was completed, Toney exclaimed, "Wow! This is incredible! I love it! It's like bringing my mother and sister back to life again. Now I can see them on my wall daily and share their stories with my family and friends."

Greg Dulan, owner of the renowned Dulan's Soul Food Restaurant in Los Angeles, envisioned his family's history displayed on the walls of his restaurant. When he saw the 40-by-60 artwork of his grandparents, beautifully restored, framed, and mounted at the heart of his restaurant, he said, "Oh my…this is beautiful! I'm so pleased. I'm almost ready to cry."

Preserving photos allows us to pass down cherished moments and stories that create a connection across generations. Photographs that capture these extraordinary stories become tangible memories—priceless pieces of life's unfolding mysteries, bridging gaps between generations. An added benefit of preserving your stories through art is the magical experience of visual storytelling, knowing that these stories will last a lifetime. Remember, life is short. Start today and preserve your family legacy because if you don't, who will?

About Ardena L. Brooks

Ardena L. Brooks is the founder and CEO of Designs by Ardena, LLC, with over 18 years of experience helping individuals and businesses preserve their history, heritage, and legacy through art. As a co-author, speaker, and master photographic artist, Ardena has assisted hundreds of clients in bringing new life to damaged and treasured photos, allowing stories captured in these images to be passed down for generations.

Ardena's services include photo restoration, portrait fine art, custom wall art, and various print media options—acrylic, aluminum, metal, and canvas—for lasting quality and durability. Ardena's unique process preserves family and cultural legacies, transforming photos into timeless art.

Based in Inglewood, California, Ardena cherishes her three adult children, a daughter-in-law, and seven grandchildren—all creative and artistically gifted. She recently lost her mother, her greatest supporter, whose memory continues to inspire her work.

Designs by Ardena is dedicated to meeting your photographic art needs, helping you capture and preserve the stories that matter most. Stay safe and be blessed. For more information, visit DesignsbyArdena.com.

NOTES

NOTES

NOTES

NOTES

THE PURPOSE OF FINANCIAL BREAKTHROUGHS

"The Ultimate Guide to Building Wealth for Your Financial Future"

Alvin Darian II

Are you ready to take control and create the life you deserve rather than simply letting life happen to you? This chapter is here to give you the push you need to start intentionally shaping your future. Like me, you must commit to investing in yourself and your future. By following *The 8 Financial Breakthroughs*, you'll be well on your way to a positive financial present and an empowered future.

The 8 Financial Breakthroughs

These 8 Financial Breakthroughs are your key to confidently building your financial foundation, transforming your relationship with money, and becoming the legacy creator you are meant to be. As you uncover your purpose and align it with your financial goals, you'll find the freedom and security you've always wanted.

Are you ready to change your financial life for the better? Let *The 8 Financial Breakthroughs* be your guide to financial independence and peace of mind. Don't let another day pass without taking control of your future—your financial breakthrough is within reach!

The 8 Financial Breakthroughs

Breakthrough 1: Financial Education

Your journey to freedom starts with building your financial education:

- Enhance your financial knowledge.

- Discover your unique financial DNA.

- Utilize financial courses and seminars to gain essential financial wisdom.

Breakthrough 2: Protection from Threats

Protecting yourself from financial threats is essential to securing your future:

- Guard against income loss with necessary insurance.

- Protect against critical and chronic illness with long-term care and life insurance.

- Shield yourself from inflation with investments that offset its impact.

- Prevent running out of funds by aligning investments with your financial goals.

- Set concrete goals and timelines to avoid procrastination.

- Minimize tax impacts through accounts like IRAs, 401(k)s, tax-loss harvesting, and Roth IRA conversions.

- Safeguard against market downturns with secure, diversified investments.

- Protect against identity theft with strong passwords and regular financial monitoring.

- Rely on trusted resources for accurate financial information.

Breakthrough 3: Cash Flow Today

Effectively managing cash flow is critical to financial stability:

- Create a budget and review automatic payments.

- Develop a plan to enhance cash flow.

- Explore new income opportunities.

- Earn through your passions.

Breakthrough 4: Debt-to-Income Ratio

Improving your debt-to-income ratio is crucial for financial health:

- Differentiate between good and bad debt.

- Increase awareness of your cash flow.

- Build and maintain a strong credit score.

Breakthrough 5: Liquidity

Enhanced liquidity provides financial flexibility:

- Keep a 6-month emergency fund.

- Maintain a 12-month fund for business opportunities and growth.

- Understand access to capital and the role of banking.

Breakthrough 6: Future Income and Net Worth

Focus on building future income and net worth:

- Develop a lifestyle and retirement plan.

- Prepare for wealth accumulation and distribution.

- Build net worth to benefit yourself, your family, and future generations.

Breakthrough 7: Legacy and Succession Plan

Create a legacy and succession plan for your family:

- Establish a life insurance trust.

- Draft a comprehensive will and trust.

- Partner with an estate attorney and CPA for effective planning.

Breakthrough 8: Accountability

Accountability ensures you achieve these financial breakthroughs:

- Select an accountability coach.

- Engage a financial professional.

- Set up a family office with a team to support wealth creation and preservation.

Following these 8 Financial Breakthroughs will empower you to take control of your financial future, build security, and become the legacy creator you deserve to be.

Build a Winning Team

I've admired sports legends like Kobe Bryant, Michael Jordan, and Muhammad Ali. Growing up playing football and basketball, I developed a work ethic influenced by my willingness to be coached to reach new heights. I love the concept of coaching; if coaching kids' sports teams paid well, I might have chosen that path. Sports teach valuable lessons—leadership, teamwork, perseverance, and the importance of being competitive and playing to win.

My mission is to help, coach, lead, and support others in becoming legends within their families, transforming their family trees for the better. I aim to be the best legacy coach, empowering 1,000 people to achieve lifetime earnings of over $1,000,000 and giving the next generation a tenfold advantage. These values drive my work and fuel my dedication to wealth-building, helping others elevate their lifestyles and realize their potential through leadership and team-building.

Winning requires a team. My focus is on fostering team-building and leadership for those who are coachable and committed to becoming legends. Becoming a legend starts with making smart financial choices, educating yourself, and leveraging those choices for your benefit. With commitment, you can take responsibility for achieving the abundant life you deserve.

A talented team, a clear vision, and a solid plan to reach your eight financial breakthroughs are essential for success in both business and life. As the Roman poet Virgil said, "Fortune sides with him who dares."

Let's Explore the Four Levels of Wealth:

- **Financial Stability**

- **Financial Security**

- **Financial Freedom**

- **Financial Abundance**

Each level contributes to your financial well-being. Now, let's dive deeper into what each level may mean for you.

Financial Stability

Reaching financial stability is a significant milestone. At this level, you can comfortably pay your bills each month. Even if there's less than $200 in your account at month's end, you aren't worried because more income is coming.

Financial Security

Financial security is a step above stability. At this level, you likely have a year's worth of savings, minimal or no credit card debt, and a stable job with little risk of layoffs. You may also have solid industry connections, so even if you lose your job, you're confident about finding another. Having these savings means you can handle emergencies, like unexpected medical expenses, without financial stress.

Financial Freedom

Financial freedom allows you to live without the constraints of financial worries. At this level, you have enough money to choose freely, whether taking a year-long vacation or pursuing a passion project. With financial freedom, you also gain the freedom of time—allowing you to decide how, where, and with whom you spend it. However, maintaining this level requires responsible financial decisions to avoid slipping back to a lower level.

Financial Abundance

Financial abundance is the highest level, where you no longer risk descending to a previous financial stage. Even if some assets lose value, your financial stability remains unaffected. Your cash flow is strong at this level, and you're free from financial concerns. Reaching financial abundance requires a mindset shift toward sustainable growth and prosperity.

Purpose of Financial Breakthroughs

The purpose of achieving these financial breakthroughs is to empower you to build a secure and abundant life. By progressing through these stages, you can shape a future where you're in control, free from financial stress, and able to align with your values and goals. Let's work together to create the financial freedom and abundance you deserve.

About Alvin Darien II

Alvin Darien, CEO of Financial Pro Network, began his journey in financial education at age 23 after earning an Electrical Engineering degree from Savannah State University. In 2003, he discovered his true calling: helping people master financial strategies and build generational wealth. Now a visionary leader with over 21 years in the industry, Alvin oversees a dedicated network of 300+ licensed financial professionals across 25+ locations nationwide.

Under Alvin's guidance, Financial Pro Network manages over $150 million in assets, has supported 10,000 clients toward financial success, and has facilitated over $300 million in legacy planning. With over 25,000 hours invested in training, research, and client support, Alvin champions transformational leadership and the growth of independent, self-reliant leaders.

Alvin's entrepreneurial spirit drives his impactful work as a speaker, trainer, and author. His books, *Don't Let Adversity Steal Your Legacy* and *The 8 Financial Breakthroughs* offer actionable insights for achieving financial freedom and building generational wealth. With a steadfast commitment to legacy-building and prosperity, Alvin has become a trusted authority in economic education.

For more information, visit FPNeducator.com.

NOTES

NOTES

NOTES

THE PURPOSE OF RECLAIMING WEALTH

Phyllis Utley

Many sacrificed for us to be where we are today. To honor their legacy and enhance and reclaim our wealth and well-being, it's essential to apply their teachings and wisdom in our lives. True wealth begins within—with self-awareness and understanding of those who came before us. The ancient mandate to "Know Thyself" remains a guiding principle. We must reclaim it.

Knowing, recording, and preserving your family history builds wealth that impacts you and future generations. This legacy supports the wealth and mental health of descendants you may never meet. By holding fast to our ancestors' dreams, we work toward true liberation and freedom and restoring the wealth taken. Let us reclaim it! Their journey, begun with blood, sweat, and tears, continues through us—they prayed for our success. We manifest their deepest aspirations, carrying them within our DNA as they live on in us. In stillness, we feel their presence and wisdom. Reclaim!

Let us uphold their dreams of freedom, liberation, and economic prosperity. We thrive with passion, humor, and style, moving forward in alignment with ancestral wisdom and joy. We restore, reclaim, and remember.

"Hold fast to dreams, for if dreams die, life is a broken-winged bird that cannot fly."
—Langston Hughes

"A people without the knowledge of their past history, origin, and culture is like a tree without roots."
—Marcus Garvey

"I had to make my own living and my own opportunity. But I made it! Don't sit down and wait for the opportunities to come. Get up and make them."
—Madam C.J. Walker

"You can't separate peace from freedom because no one can be at peace without his freedom."
—Malcolm X

"When I dare to be powerful and use my strength in the service of my vision, then it becomes less and less important whether I am afraid."
—Audre Lorde

"The new dawn blooms as we free it / For there is always light, / if only we're brave enough to see it / If only we're brave enough to be it."
—Amanda Gorman

Our ancestors faced many fears head-on, and their strength enhanced our own as we learned from them. It increased our power, wealth, and majesty. We feel and know that we are not alone; we have an entourage of heroes behind us, beside us, and ahead of us. They have passed the baton to us, and we move forward with it in hand to reclaim.

Mansa Musa (Musa I of Mali) ruled the kingdom of Mali from 1312 C.E. to 1337 C.E. Under his reign, Mali became one of Africa's wealthiest kingdoms, and Mansa Musa was among the most affluent individuals in history. When adjusted for inflation, his net worth is estimated to have been around $400 billion. With this legacy ingrained in our psyche, we cannot help but win. This awareness propels us to achieve great and mighty things.

We all experience nervous anxiety and fear. Sometimes, fear can even derail us from living our best lives. However, when you live authentically and act in a way that serves your highest good, the possibility of fear and failure doesn't seem so overwhelming.

You know your ancestors faced fear and overcame it. Because of them, you are where you are today, and humanity is better for it. Fear becomes less significant when you walk in knowing your truth and those who came before you. You acknowledge it, experience it, and say, "Hey, I see you…thank you for coming by," then keep moving forward. Fear can no longer stifle you, derail you from action, or create analysis paralysis. You feel it within and press on.

You are more than a conqueror, just as those who came before you were. Each new day, we build wealth, and you feel the cry of victory. Your birthday celebrations testify to their rebirth within you with every breath. Our health is our wealth. We were born to thrive, not merely survive. It is so because we declare and decree it so. Our ancestors smile upon us, loving our journey of wealth reclamation and building. It begins within and manifests outwardly. We are who we've been waiting for. We have the keys to unlock the door. Victory is ours to rebuild, restore, reimagine, remember, and reclaim. We are on the move.

Once upon a time, a Copper Colored American Indian rejoiced in sharing the stories and principles her ancestors lived by. Her heart danced to the memories of the warriors, healers, and builders who came before her. She recognized that she had been miseducated in the finest colonial schools in the country. She knew that the images of Indigenous people in the media had whitewashed her people, impacted by paper genocide. It is imperative to understand that the tens of millions of Native Americans who disappeared after 1492 did not all die in the "holocaust." Many thousands were sent to Europe and Africa—a history seldom taught in schools.

Moreover, many disappeared in plain sight, absorbed into the enslaved population and reclassified as Colored, Negro, and, by the 1980s, African American. She encourages all people to learn their history. Whatever your family's story, gather the jewels. Learn the lessons that will fuel your decisions. Great joy comes from knowing the life lessons of those who came before you; their wisdom lives on in you, increasing your wealth quotient.

I am a Copper-Colored American Indian. Daily, I learn more about those who came before me, apply their knowledge to my life, face my fears, and move forward. As my Momma used to say, "Keep going." She also said, "Celebrate—you got this." I am a co-creator of great and precious gifts for the world, increasing my overflow. You can't stop the flow.

I can feel her embrace. I can smell the collard greens she had on the stove, freshly picked from the backyard garden, where she grew basil, onions, okra, potatoes, kale, and cabbage. I say thank you to my dear Momma. "All the things you planted, sowed, and hoped for—I witnessed their manifestation." I reclaim it. My Momma, lovingly known as Queen Mother Maggie Belle, lived in Asheville, NC, and transitioned from this life in 2021. She believed everyone should have good food, and she started a café called *12 Baskets,* which still serves food and provides free groceries. I love to see people enjoying the delicious food. I feel the wealth.

You, too, can create a family heritage book and interview family members to preserve their wisdom. Oral history is a wealth of knowledge, a testimony of personal experiences. Ask questions and enjoy the journey. Our family members hold a wealth of knowledge that enhances our "wealth-being." Remember to have fun and treasure the moments to master wealth, health, and wealth-building as you reclaim!

About Phyllis Utley

Phyllis Utley is a Wealth Reclamation Practitioner dedicated to expanding social capital and wealth-building through art and family history. Recognized as one of Asheville's Hidden Influencers by *Mountain Xpress* in 2017, Phyllis also had the honor of collaborating with Nobel Peace Prize laureate Leymah Gbowee at Columbia University's Women, Peace, and Security Program in 2018, which highlights local women catalysts for change across the country. She is a Tzedek Community Impact Award recipient and actively supports the Reparations Movement to promote community healing with lasting impact. Phyllis serves on the board of "United for a Fair Economy," where she guides individuals with wealth and class privilege toward actions of redistribution, atonement, and repair of ancestral harms. Listen to *Dismantling Economic Oppression: A Deep Dive into Reparations* on major podcast platforms.

NOTES

NOTES

NOTES

THE PURPOSE OF GRIEF

MiaMichelle Henry

Grief shatters the foundation of our lives, exposing truths we might have overlooked. It shakes our souls, uncovering hidden emotions and reshaping how we see ourselves and those we love. As we face grief, we begin to see it as both a challenge and a growth path. I offer practical tools to help navigate this chaos, guiding us toward renewal. Through this journey, we discover that grief, while painful, can lead to a deeper, more meaningful life filled with love and understanding.

Grief is a natural and inevitable part of life. It touches us all, whether it's the loss of a loved one, the end of a significant relationship, or a major life change. But grief isn't just about loss—it's about transformation. It's a powerful force that can reshape us, teach us resilience, and guide us toward a deeper understanding of ourselves and the world around us. This chapter will explore how embracing grief can lead to profound personal growth and new beginnings.

I was the woman everyone thought had it all together—a mental health professional and business owner admired for my service to the community. I was constantly chasing the next goal, the next achievement. Yet, beneath the facade, I was silently grappling with my own grief, too profound to voice. Life has a way of changing everything in an instant. I had spent years guiding clients through grief, knowing it's a journey filled with stages that can stretch out for years.

Then, life changed everything in an instant. I lost my mother to cancer. She was my anchor, guiding light, and most significant source of wisdom. I will never forget those words: "It's terminal." We had just celebrated her 75th birthday. She didn't even look sick, but we lost her three months after those words were spoken. Her loss hit me like a freight train, shattering the foundation of my life and leaving me in a sea of sorrow. Yet, being the professional I am, I buried my grief beneath layers of work and responsibilities. I told myself I didn't have time to grieve; I needed to keep moving forward. And so I did—pushing through the pain, plastering on a smile, convincing myself that I was strong enough to handle it all.

But the truth was, I felt dead inside. The loss of my mother created a void that no amount of work or success could fill. I felt disconnected from myself, my purpose, and the life I once loved. It was as if the essence of who I am had been stripped away, leaving me lost and exhausted.

As a counselor, I knew I had to use the very practices I teach others to bring myself back from the heartbreak of my loss. One of the first steps on my healing journey was grounding myself in the present moment. I turned to ground exercises—simple practices that connected me to the earth and helped me feel more rooted. Walking barefoot on the grass, feeling the earth beneath my feet, and taking deep breaths in nature became my way of anchoring myself in an unsteady reality. This practice, though simple, profoundly affected my sense of well-being.

I also leaned on breathwork, a tool I often recommend to clients to release stuck emotions. I would sit quietly, close my eyes, and take slow, deep breaths, visualizing the pain leaving my body with each exhale. It was like a gentle wave washing over me, carrying away the grief that had been trapped inside. This practice didn't just bring me peace—it allowed me to release the tension in my body, bringing me a sense of calm I hadn't felt in years.

Affirmations, another powerful tool, became a crucial part of my healing journey. Inspired by the teachings of Louise Hay, I began to incorporate positive affirmations into my daily routine. I would say to myself, "I am safe to feel my emotions," "I release the pain of the past," and "I am worthy of love and healing." These affirmations helped me reframe my thoughts, shifting my focus from pain to healing and self-compassion. They created a more positive and supportive internal dialogue that nurtured my spirit rather than tearing it down.

Movement, too, became a vital part of my healing process. I knew the importance of expressing emotions physically and applied this knowledge to myself. Through dance, yoga, or simply walking mindfully, I found that moving my body allowed me to release my suppressed emotions. Dance, in particular, became my sanctuary. I would close my eyes, play my favorite music, and let my body move freely, releasing whatever emotions arose in the moment. This practice wasn't just about physical exercise; it was a form of therapy, a way to process my grief and celebrate my resilience.

I noticed a shift in my perspective through all these practices—grounding, breathwork, affirmations, and movement. I no longer saw my grief as something to be avoided or suppressed; instead, I saw it as a powerful force for transformation. My mother's passing had not broken me—it had opened me up to a deeper understanding of myself, my purpose, and my capacity for love and healing.

I realized that my purpose wasn't just about my career or achievements; it was about living true to myself, honoring my values, positively impacting the world, and living a life filled with love and joy. Embracing my grief allowed me to reconnect with my body, release the pain I had been carrying, and cultivate a sense of inner peace. I began to see my life in a new light, not defined by external success but by my ability to live authentically and embrace my humanity.

In the end, the journey of grief taught me that true strength isn't about enduring everything on your own—it's about being honest with yourself, embracing your vulnerability, and seeking the help you need. It's about using your experiences as a catalyst for growth and transformation. My mother's loss was profound, but it led me to a deeper sense of purpose and fulfillment than I had ever known before.

As I reflect on my journey, I encourage others to embrace the lessons that grief offers. Whether through somatic therapy, breathwork, affirmations, or simply allowing yourself to feel your emotions, remember that healing is a process that requires patience, self-compassion, and a willingness to be open to the possibilities that lie ahead. Just as I found my way to a new chapter of life, so can you find your path to healing, purpose, and fulfillment.

About MiaMichelle Henry

MiaMichelle Henry is a dynamic entrepreneur, educator, author, therapist, business coach, and Les Brown Platinum Speaker. Known for her captivating presence and practical guidance, she inspires individuals, couples, organizations, and communities to pursue authenticity and success.

With 28 years in entrepreneurship and relationship coaching, MiaMichelle skillfully blends accountability with transformative strategies to guide clients in their personal and professional growth. As CEO and Founder of Rita Rose Academy and Urban Sage Counseling and Wellness, MiaMichelle fosters emotional literacy and well-being for families and children, integrating her knowledge of childhood development and mental health.

MiaMichelle's dedication to community impact is evident in her company's $1 million donation to support accessible childcare and over 10,000 volunteer hours. She has collaborated with Percy "Master P" Miller on this work, *Mastering Wealth: Volume 2 Purpose*, and is set to release her book, *Sacred Paths: Timeless Wisdom for Business Legacy*.

MiaMichelle's podcast, Soulful Exhale™, offers transformative conversations on mental wellness, relationships, and entrepreneurship. It encourages listeners to find peace, purpose, and passion in today's busy world. Passionate about lifelong growth, she finds joy in time spent with her family, traveling, reading, and dancing.

NOTES

NOTES

NOTES

THE PURPOSE OF CURBING EMOTIONAL SPENDING

Aaron W. Smith

Accredited Investment Fiduciary

I was seated behind my desk while Dr. C sat across from me, weeping, ignoring the nearby box of tissues and cup of tea she'd accepted upon arrival. She was elegantly dressed, her hair in a stylish Afro, with an array of diamond studs along an earlobe. She tried unsuccessfully to continue reading aloud the letter that her mother had written years earlier, encouraging her to work with me on securing her financial future. Dr. C's parents – her dad worked as a janitor at a school near my Fairfax, Virginia office, and her mother as an elementary school teacher. Both had passed away. Dr. C, the daughter they conceived after decades of praying for her, was keeping the promise she'd made to them to do something about her finances.

"I'm so ashamed," Dr. C said.

"Why ashamed?" I asked.

In helping clients create financial wealth, I encourage them to consider their emotions regarding spending and saving. During 31 years of service with my wife, Pat, and as founders of the A.W. Smith Financial Group, we've learned that mental health -- emotional, psychological, and social well-being--largely determines how people handle money.

Dr. C. explained that during decades as a public speaking coach in Los Angeles, she'd taught clients how to present themselves as prime-time ready. I recalled her parents' pride in her success, but her mother once confided her concern about their daughter's lavish spending.

Dr. C stated, "I'm ashamed because I've spent everything I've earned and more. I'm in debt. My parents always put the best spin on my situation, even when I borrowed from them."

I told her that she was ahead of many of my first-time clients. Why? Many people must pay more attention to their finances and emotional states, leaving them unprepared for the future. While my work focuses on African Americans, poor financial preparation is an issue for people from all racial backgrounds. In 2022, U.S. household debt rose to $16.9 trillion, an increase of $2.75 trillion since 2019, according to the Federal Reserve. That's $986 billion in credit card debt, $1.55 trillion in car loans, and $1.6 trillion in student loans. Black households are far more likely to have unsecured debt, especially student loans and medical debts.[3] That means they're not backed by collateral and, therefore, riskier for the lender, so they carry higher interest rates.

Some people explain these differences by judging us based on race. Longtime *Washington Post* financial columnist Michelle Singletary writes of being raised with four siblings by her grandmother, who struggled to keep them and their home presentable despite a modest income. Singletary recalls a welfare worker arriving to inspect their Baltimore rowhouse and deciding that the family didn't look "needy enough" for cash assistance.

Black people are often viewed by others as spendthrifts, often without taking into account the so-called U.S. 'Wealth Gap.' Black families' median and mean wealth remains at less than 15 percent of that of white families. That substantial gap is tied to historical and contemporary factors, which include:

1. Racist housing policies have empowered white American wealth creation while denying access to the same path to African Americans.

2. Lower inheritance percentages: An estimated 30 percent of white families but only 10 percent of Black families in the U.S. have received financial inheritances.

3. Racial wage income differences

4. Restrictive market and banking policies.

I'm proud to say that despite roadblocks, millions of African Americans have created wealth, and some of them, including some of my clients, can be described as "super savers." This was not the case for Dr. C. In her career, she'd earned a "great deal," but she had spent most of it to look the part so she could get the part... the position...the next contract.

---

3   Briana Sullivan, Donald Hays, and Neil Bennett, "Households With a White, Non-Hispanic Householder Were Ten Times Wealthier Than Those With a Black Householder in 2021," April 23, 2024, United States Census Bureau, https://www.census.gov/library/stories/2024/04/wealth-by-race.html.

Her tears of shame reflected her regret for overspending and avoiding her mother's request to begin working with me to build wealth. The good news was that she was determined to make a fresh start. During our work together, I encouraged her to clarify what she owed, develop a plan to pay her debts, start saving and investing, and start journaling about her financial/emotional experiences that fed her sense of shame.

Other clients have talked with me about feelings of regret, anger, helplessness, hopelessness, etc., and many find relief in journaling. I also offer them numerous suggestions to support new spending habits to help develop a sense of relief and clarity about the road ahead. Even small initial steps can help to feed momentum by relieving constant financial stress. In achieving initial financial goals, they develop a sense of empowerment and begin to grasp that they can create for themselves financial freedom. I describe their recovery as going from feeling 'black and blue' (battered and worn down) to *In the Black,* a financial term that refers to overcoming out-of-control debt and building wealth.[4]

One example of the importance of understanding emotions and personal finance involves the term 'reaction formation,' which refers to thoughts and impulses that cause exaggerated behaviors that obscure what an individual might feel. It is not unusual for someone's behavior to express the opposite of their true feelings. For example, some might convince themselves they deserve to spend whatever they want to feel that they *are* enough, which only temporarily distracts them from their impoverished sense of self. Journaling to recognize hurtful feelings, emotions, and experiences and individual or group therapeutic support can be highly effective for strengthening self-awareness and staving off impulsive financial decisions.

I close with more suggestions for wealth-building opportunities:

1. If you feel the urge to spend on something you cannot afford and can do without, ask yourself (perhaps in journal writing) whether this purchase is something you desire so you don't have to worry about your present circumstances – or to feel better about something that happened in the past? When possible, take a walk outside and breathe deeply. Consider what it

---

4 The latter of these is also the title of my book: *In the Black: Live Faithfully, Prosper Financially,* written with Brenda Lane Richardson (Harper Collins, 2009).

means to live in the present – in your body, which is empowered by your spirit. Breathe. Wiggle your toes and fingers. Our emotional selves can pull us backward to a time of unhappiness or forward to worry about the future. Refuse to be pulled off-center. Remind yourself: Your life is in the here and now. You are enough.

2. Are you feeling frightened about bills? Diversify your income. In this gig economy, finding additional work opportunities, such as Lyft drivers, meal delivery drivers, or customers' telephone orders for a catalog company, is easier than ever. Use part-time additional income to pay down debt, save, and invest.

3. Are you short of cash and considering withdrawing from your 401(k) or 403(b)? By thinking creatively, fight the urge to withdraw from these tax-advantaged employer-sponsored retirement plans. For instance, the 'k' in 401(k) is associated with an Internal Revenue Code. But it might help to imagine it as an abbreviation for 'kiss' because this financial instrument deserves some love, and here's an example of why: A 30-year-old earning $85,000 per year who contributes three percent to a 401(k) with standard contributions along with an employer's match ... would have a return of $949, 121 by the age 65, assuming average annual returns of eight percent.

4. Feeling broke and alone because you're saving money and don't get out much? Invite friends over for a 'broke' party, complete with inexpensive snacks. Play cards, dance, and have fun without expense. An even cheaper alternative is starting 'no-spend' meetings on Zoom. Feeling connected to others can lower stress.

5. Invite folks to join you for monthly meetings at one another's homes (not restaurants or clubs) so you can share tips about savings and work opportunities.

6. If you cannot stop spending, order a copy of *How to Get Out of Debt, Stay Out of Debt, and Live Prosperously*, which is based on the principles and techniques of Debtors Anonymous. And join an online or in-person Debtors Anonymous Support group. To find a meeting, google Debtors Anonymous.

Good news: Dr C has paid off most of her debts and is building wealth. I recently reminded her of one of her mother's favorite verses from Isaiah 25: "…neither shall there be mourning, nor crying, nor pain anymore, for the former things have passed away."

About Aaron Smith

Richmond native Aaron W. Smith is a celebrated author, media personality, radio host, entrepreneur, motivational speaker, and financial expert with 31 years of experience serving individuals, business owners, and professional athletes. He holds a Bachelor of Arts from the University of Richmond, majoring in Sociology with a minor in Economics. He also earned his MBA from the University of Richmond and Accredited Investment Fiduciary certification from the University of Pittsburgh.

Aaron is the author of In the Black: Live Faithfully, Prosper Financially—The Ultimate 9-Step Plan for Financial Fitness and On the Line, a guide for entrepreneurs. He has appeared with Brian Williams as a guest on WRIC-8 (ABC), WTVR6 (CBS), Arise America, NPR, and NBC Nightly News. His expertise has also been featured in numerous national and regional publications, including *Forbes*, *Black Enterprise*, *Investment News*, *USA Today*, *Inside Business*, *The Richmond Free Press*, *The Richmond Times-Dispatch*, *Financial Advisor*, and *Dow Jones NewsWire*.

Aaron is married to Patricia Smith and is the father of Jasmine Wiggins and Justin Smith. He has one granddaughter, Kinsley Arin Wiggins. For more information, visit g2gwealth.com.

NOTES

NOTES

NOTES

NOTES

THE PURPOSE OF BLACK-OWNED K-12 EDUCATION

Lisa Watson

Imagine a Black-owned K-12 education economy: a network of independent Black-owned micro-schools housed within America's 85,000 Black churches, which currently sit empty 90% of the time. These independent "one-room schoolhouses" would be dedicated to educating America's 7.7 million Black students. These schools would be founded on principles such as Proverbs 22:6, "Train up a child in the way he should go, and when he is old, he will not depart from it," and Malcolm X's assertion, "Only a fool would allow his enemy to educate his kids."

The United States has 99,000 government schools versus 330,000 churches (85,000 Black-owned). Think about that: Black America has nearly as many churches as the government has schools. Imagine the impact of 85,000 Black-owned schools on closing the achievement gap, bridging the wealth gap, increasing financial literacy, expanding entrepreneurship, reducing crime, eliminating the obesity epidemic, and strengthening the Black family. As the church has been the historical heart of the Black community for over 300 years, it serves as the perfect foundation upon which to launch the HBCUs K-12 initiative.

It's official—school choice has gone mainstream. Thirty-five states have passed meaningful school-choice legislation, and recent Supreme Court rulings have strengthened parental rights over K-12 education funding. In Espinoza v. Montana Department of Revenue (2020), the Supreme Court held that states cannot prevent families participating in school-choice programs from selecting religiously affiliated schools, invalidating Blaine amendments in 37 states that barred public funds from attending religious schools. In Carson v. Makin (2022), the Court ruled that Maine's exclusion of religious schools from state-sponsored choice programs was unconstitutional. At this rate, it's conceivable that in 100 years, when their great-grandparents talk about failing government schools, the great-grandkids will ask, *Wait, what? The government used to run schools?*

School choice offers K-12 education options, allowing families to choose alternatives to zip-code-assigned public schools, such as private, charter, hybrid, homeschooling, or public schools in other districts. Funding mechanisms vary by state, including tax credits, education savings accounts, or vouchers. The "Gold Standard," known as "Money Follows the Child," allocates a tuition amount for families to choose a school—or pool resources to build private schools or homeschool co-ops.

School choice legislation could fund a network of Black-owned K-12 schools, joining the 34,000+ private schools already in the U.S. While Black Americans make up 14% of the population, they control less than 2% of the private school sector. School choice has the potential to desegregate private school ownership because Black lives won't truly matter until Black minds matter.

The 17th century is calling, and it wants its school system back. America's first public school, Boston Latin, was founded in 1635. While every other "invention" since then has evolved dramatically, not much has changed in nearly 400 years of government-sponsored education. Imagine the Wright Brothers' first single-engine plane with its 59-second flight—now imagine the space shuttle. Think of Alexander Graham Bell's first telephone, with its wires, transmitter, and receiver—now think of your smartphone. Or Philo Farnsworth's first television with its 3-inch screen— now picture the massive screens covering skyscrapers in Times Square. These leaps happened because industries embraced the marketplace.

Meanwhile, government schools still rely on teachers standing before blackboards, with students sitting at desks memorizing facts and formulas. And just as the original airplane, telephone, and television are obsolete, so is our centuries-old method of educating kids. Government schools are not failing by accident; they are failing by design.

America's 50 million students (7.7 million Black students) deserve customized K-12 options. The micro-school revolution offers that solution. Private schools for the elite and failing schools for the poor are un-American. Like the iconic line from *The Six Million Dollar Man*, "We can rebuild it. We have the technology," we have the resources: 85,000 church buildings and school-choice funding. Rather than 99,000 government school warehouses, we can build one million one-room schoolhouses.

The concept of Black America taking responsibility for education—from teacher hiring and curriculum to food systems and disciplinary practices—is not new. The first Historically Black College or University (HBCU), Cheyney University (originally The Institute for Colored Youth), was founded in 1837 by former slave-owner Richard Humphreys. Today, over 100 HBCUs produce 75% of Black PhDs, 40% of Black engineers, 50% of Black teachers, 70% of Black doctors and dentists, 75% of Black military officers, and 80% of Black federal judges.

Even more inspiring, iconic educator and Tuskegee Institute founder Booker T. Washington partnered with Sears executive Julius Rosenwald to build around 5,000 one-room schoolhouses throughout the rural South between 1912 and 1932. These "Rosenwald Schools" educated over 700,000 Black students between 1912 and 1973. The blueprint for change exists—it's time to use it.

An economy is "a system or range of interrelated monetary activities related to production, consumption, and financial activities within a country, region, or community." The purpose of free markets is to allocate financial resources among participants within the economy. In his book *Powernomics*, Dr. Claud Anderson, former Assistant Secretary in the Commerce Department, links the wealth-building success of a culture to "bouncing money." The more times a dollar circulates within a community, the greater its wealth. Dr. Anderson notes that Jewish communities circulate money 18 times; white communities 8-12; Asian and Arab communities 13-14; Hispanic communities 6-7; but Black America, zero times. Because money exits the Black community so quickly, the result is entrenched poverty and powerlessness. In 2023, the government K-12 education economy topped $1 trillion, yet almost none is retained within the Black community due to a lack of business ownership. School-choice legislation could change this.

Here's the blueprint: reframing school-choice funding as 21st-century reparations to support a network of independent K-12 schools. The education voucher would circulate through Black-owned entities—from parents to schools, to hiring teachers and contracting with Black-owned businesses (HVAC, janitorial services, food services, landscaping, bus drivers, uniforms, curriculum). Controlling curriculum would be transformative, allowing HBCU-led K-12 schools to teach STEM, financial literacy, entrepreneurship, urban gardening, and essential life skills. This model is designed to circulate money 6-9 times within the community.

The math is simple: 85,000 Black churches × 7.7 million Black students = 91 students per micro-school. With a $5,000 tuition allocation, each micro-school could operate with a $455,000 budget. The traditional one-room schoolhouse model— one teacher, multiple grades, and competency-based learning—would fit well within the HBCU K-12 framework. At its core, a micro-school could be a teacher, 10-20 students, a screen for digital resources, community volunteers, and free or low-cost curriculum options. Volunteers could teach practical skills: realtors on home buying, car salespeople on purchasing vehicles, loan officers on credit and mortgage basics, and bankers on savings fundamentals. HBCU K-12 could revive essential, real-world training, mirroring the successful 180-year track record of HBCUs—demonstrating that if our ancestors built colleges, we could build kindergartens.

About Lisa Watson

Lisa Watson, a former social justice warrior turned education activist, is on a mission to reform failing schools. As the first in her family to graduate from college with a B.A. in Psychology and Political Science, her access to quality K-12 education gave her the escape velocity needed to break the cycle of poverty. However, she recognizes that this pathway remains out of reach for students trapped in underperforming, zip-code-based schools.

A natural-born activist, Lisa's social justice credentials include roles as a Planned Parenthood intern, Union Steward, ACLU Affiliate Board member, Co-Chair of the ACLU Racial Justice Task Force, ACLU Affirmative Action Officer, ACLU Kansas City Chapter President, and ACLU National Board member in NYC. Now guided by Frederick Douglass's mantra, "I will unite with anybody to do right, and nobody to do wrong," and driven by the conviction that Black lives won't truly matter until Black minds matter, Lisa seeks to educate Americans—especially Black Americans—that access to quality K-12 education is the civil rights issue of the 21st century.

Lisa's movement, The Education Equality Revolution, aims to replicate the success of Historically Black Colleges and Universities (HBCUs) by stating, "If our ancestors could build colleges, we can build kindergartens."

NOTES

NOTES

NOTES

THE PURPOSE OF RESILIENCE: BUILDING UNBREAKABLE STRENGTH

Reginald K. Harris, PhD

What Is Resilience?

> *"Do not judge me by my success; judge me by how many times I fell and got back up again."*
> *— Nelson Mandela*

Resilience is the ability to recover from a traumatic event, allowing you to return to normalcy after an unexpected circumstance has thrown you off course. This may arise from financial setbacks, the loss of a loved one, a breakup, physical illness, or any other event that essentially knocks you off your feet.

Resilience is crucial to achieving your life's purpose. A lack of resilience can lead to a life filled with wish lists and verbalized dreams that never manifest. Resilience is not typically innate but is cultivated through experience, learning, and perseverance. Each setback presents an opportunity to build resilience, transforming challenges into stepping stones toward a more purposeful, empowered life.

Developing resilience strengthens one's ability to face future obstacles and enhances confidence in navigating life's unpredictable paths. It is the foundation upon which personal growth, achievement, and fulfillment are built, guiding one toward realizing one's highest potential.

The principles in this chapter are designed to equip you with resilience, a skill you can apply to all areas of your life. These insights are drawn from decades of empirical research and personal experiences. They are intended to increase your probability of living the purposeful, thriving life God has destined for you.

Set the Right Expectations

> *"Everybody has a plan until they get punched in the mouth."- Mike Tyson*

The first step to increasing resilience is setting a realistic plan for how your life may unfold. Your expectations play a crucial role in your ability to handle challenging events. Developing an awareness that things can go wrong isn't pessimism; it's a practical approach that prepares you for life's inevitable ups and downs. In my personal life, I expect the best but always prepare for the worst. Balancing hope with preparedness allows me to face outcomes that differ from my hopes and prayers without feeling as though I have personally failed.

A term often used today is "pivot"—in other words, be ready to take an alternative route to reach the same goal. The greatest disappointment usually stems from unrealistic expectations that nothing will go wrong. Setting a realistic life plan includes understanding that the journey to your "best life" may involve unexpected turns and detours, but these don't require abandoning your original dream.

As a Christian, my worldview is anchored in Romans 8:28: "All things work together for good to those that love God." This belief has guided me as I have seen God's work repeatedly unfold. Because of my faith and obedience to Him, I trust everything will work out even when unfavorable circumstances appear.

Counseling individuals who have lost loved ones is always challenging. Still, it becomes even more complicated when the loss occurs through traumatic events such as car accidents, murder, or natural disasters. While some people face these sudden tragedies with a perspective of gratitude amidst despair, most are understandably overwhelmed by the shock of their loss.

The following insights are not meant to diminish the profound grief that comes with losing a parent, spouse, or child. Instead, they offer a way to prepare mentally for the worst-case scenario. Each day brings the possibility of life and, equally, the chance of loss; acknowledging this can help us prepare mentally for unexpected events. I have mentally imagined the funerals of those I love to prepare myself, as much as possible, for life without them. This may seem harsh, but as a Christian, I am committed to fulfilling God's will in my life, regardless of what may come.

By identifying my life's purpose as fulfilling God's will, I have mentally prepared myself to handle adversity without losing sight of this purpose. This mindset helps me stay resilient and determined to persevere until my life's work is completed.

Illusion of Control

You can make many plans, but the Lord's purpose will prevail. -Proverbs 19:21 NLT

The illusion of total control over life is a mirage that can hinder the pursuit of one's dreams. While some people struggle more with control issues than others, nearly everyone desires some degree of control over their lives. For those with an extreme need to control everything, this often stems from past trauma, such as low self-esteem or experiences where they felt powerless. This desire to control may serve as a defense mechanism to prevent them from ever feeling vulnerable again. Conversely, those with an external locus of control believe everything is someone else's responsibility. This lack of accountability can also lead to adverse outcomes. However, here, we focus on individuals who believe total control is within their grasp.

People with a heightened sense of control often face intense difficulties when confronted with traumatic events. They may think their meticulous planning, financial status, or ability to manipulate environments with intellect or charisma can secure every outcome. When reality disrupts this illusion, it can derail their lives, potentially taking years or even decades to recover—if they recover at all.

One example is a young woman I counseled who struggled with maintaining relationships because she couldn't tolerate any missteps that didn't fit into her list of acceptable behaviors. She is far from alone in this struggle, as many single women today face similar challenges in finding lasting relationships due to control issues. This example highlights how the illusion of control can prevent people from achieving their dream of a lifelong partnership.

Ultimately, the only choices you can truly control are your own; others' decisions remain theirs alone. Though this may seem simplistic, it's a vital reflection for anyone who believes everything should align with their desires. The inability to be flexible on the journey to success can make even the slightest obstacle seem insurmountable, undermining hope in achieving goals—whether in business, relationships, or other areas of life.

About Reginald K. Harris, PhD

Dr. Reginald K. Harris is an entrepreneur, minister, and transformational speaker dedicated to empowering people to lead purpose-driven lives. With over 2 decades of entrepreneurial experience, he operates Harris Realty, Tennessee's second-largest independently Black-owned real estate firm, and manages a commercial real estate development company, Greenwood1. Beyond real estate, Dr. Harris serves as a staff pastor, mentor, and board member for various nonprofit organizations.

Dr. Harris holds a Bachelor's degree in Psychology from Xavier University in Louisiana and a Master's in Curriculum and instruction and Counseling. He earned his doctorate in International Psychology with a concentration in Organizations and Systems from the Chicago School of Professional Psychology.

Although he wears many hats, Dr. Harris believes his most important role is as a devoted man of faith. His wife and three children are his highest priority, and his Christian principles form the foundation upon which he has built his life and career. For more information, visit ReginaldKHarris.com.

NOTES

NOTES

NOTES

THE PURPOSE OF BUILDING GENERATIONAL WEALTH THROUGH REAL ESTATE

LaToshia Hall

Building generational wealth through real estate is not a new concept. History shows that some wealthiest Americans—like Rockefeller, J.P. Morgan, and Vanderbilt—built their fortunes on real estate. However, for Black Americans, this type of wealth-building holds particular significance due to systemic inequalities and the enduring legacy of racial discrimination. For centuries, Black Americans have faced redlining, economic exclusion, and restricted access to wealth-building opportunities, primarily through real estate. These barriers have significantly contributed to the racial wealth gap, as the lack of Black community investment in homeownership remains a critical factor.

As of July 2024, only 45% of Black Americans own homes compared to 75% of white Americans. Alarmingly, when the Fair Housing Act passed in 1968, Black homeownership stood at 41%. Over the past 56 years, there has been only a 4% increase in Black homeownership, highlighting the persistent barriers to achieving this fundamental step toward economic stability. This disparity is a driving force behind the widening wealth gap between Black Americans and their white counterparts.

Barriers to Black Homeownership

Why are Black Americans still facing the same challenges after decades of advocacy? Having worked in real estate for over 20 years, I've witnessed Black buyers' unique struggles. Even as recently as five years ago, studies showed that Black mortgage applicants were significantly more likely to be denied than their white counterparts, even when their financial profiles were identical, with race being the only differentiator. Additionally, many Black families lack the necessary savings for a down payment due to rising rental costs and other living expenses that erode disposable income. Compounding this issue are decades of predatory lending, redlining, and exclusionary zoning practices, all of which have hindered Black Americans' ability to achieve homeownership.

Why Real Estate Matters for Generational Wealth

Homeownership has historically been a cornerstone of wealth accumulation in the United States. Families can build equity, establish community roots, and pass assets to future generations. For Black families, investing in real estate can create tangible wealth, provide a passive income stream, and establish financial stability.

Building wealth through real estate also allows one to break the cycle of poverty, creating intergenerational prosperity. By acquiring and managing real estate, Black families can create a legacy that empowers future generations. This wealth transfer can serve as a tool to bridge the racial wealth gap, offering children and grandchildren the resources to pursue their dreams and achieve economic mobility.

Real Estate as a Tool for Empowerment

Real estate offers financial independence and control over one's economic destiny that few other investments can match. Unlike traditional employment or investments subject to external forces, real estate allows individuals to make strategic decisions, diversify portfolios, and build long-term wealth. By leveraging financing options, managing properties, and actively engaging with the market, Black homeowners and investors can create sustainable income and secure their families' futures for future generations.

Beyond personal financial gain, real estate investing can drive community empowerment and revitalization. Black real estate investors can play a vital role in revitalizing neighborhoods, supporting local businesses, and preserving affordable housing. These investments can combat gentrification, ensuring Black families remain rooted in their communities as property values rise. Real estate investments can create lasting social and economic change by fostering economic growth, job creation, and pride in ownership.

Educating Future Generations

The key to sustaining generational wealth lies in financial literacy and teaching younger generations the value of real estate. Understanding the complexities of the real estate market and the importance of holding onto inherited property is essential. Land is an irreplaceable resource, and its value only increases over time. With this knowledge, families can avoid losing assets to predatory investors who exploit market dynamics to acquire property at undervalued rates. Educating youth early about real estate can pave the way for a future where wealth continues to grow within the Black community.

Conclusion

The importance of building generational wealth through real estate for Black Americans cannot be overstated. Real estate offers a pathway to economic empowerment, social equity, and long-term financial stability. By overcoming historical barriers and investing in property, Black individuals can create a lasting legacy of prosperity that uplifts families and communities. Through strategic planning, education, and a commitment to long-term wealth-building, Black Americans can build a brighter, more equitable future for themselves and future generations.

About LaToshia Hall

With over 22 years of experience in the real estate industry, LaToshia Hall is a dedicated and client-focused real estate professional committed to helping buyers, sellers, and investors achieve their goals. Her in-depth knowledge of the local market, strong negotiation skills, and meticulous attention to detail allow her to provide personalized, strategic guidance to clients throughout the buying or selling process.

Whether you're a first-time homebuyer, a seasoned investor, or looking to sell your property, LaToshia offers expert advice, exceptional service, and a seamless real estate experience. Her passion for real estate, unwavering integrity, and dedication to client satisfaction make her an ideal partner for all your real estate needs.

As a REALTOR® with Powerhouse Realty Inc. in Greater Jacksonville, FL, LaToshia is ready to help turn your real estate dreams into reality. Let's work together to make your vision a success!

NOTES

NOTES

NOTES

NOTES

THE PURPOSE OF FISHING IN DIGITAL WATERS

"Casting Your Net in the Right Pond for Business Success"

Sharyn Faison-Williams

Introduction

A *nd it came to pass in the process of time, that the king of Egypt died, and the children of Israel sighed because of their bondage, and their cry came up unto God. And God heard their groaning, and God looked upon the children of Israel, and God had respect unto them.*

Just as Moses was chosen as a beacon of hope to guide the Israelites in their darkest hour, we hope to be a guiding light for small and medium-sized business owners at Grace Sixty Marketing Agency. We understand the sleepless nights spent worrying about where the next customer will come from, and we are here to transform those concerns into opportunities through the power of digital marketing.

Our mission is to help you turn your business into the thriving entity you've always envisioned. In a world filled with potential, digital marketing is the pond where your opportunities flourish. We believe in empowering our clients, not just by offering services but by teaching them to succeed. The adage goes, "If you give a person a fish, you feed them for a day. If you teach them to fish, you feed them for a lifetime." At Grace Sixty, we go further—we show you where to cast your net.

Imagine your business surviving and thriving—drawing in an abundant "catch" of customers eager to engage with your brand. Like the fishermen in Luke 5 who toiled all night but caught nothing until they followed divine guidance, we aim to help you transform your efforts into success.

Digital marketing is more than a tool; it's the bridge connecting your vision with your audience. With tailored strategies, creative solutions, and data-driven insights, we equip you with the skills and knowledge to build lasting customer relationships that have sustained your business for years.

As we embark on this journey together, remember that just as God respected the cries of the children of Israel, we respect your dreams and aspirations. Let us guide you toward the promised land of success, where every effort yields abundant rewards.

The Power of Paid Advertising

In today's competitive digital landscape, paid advertising has emerged as a powerful tool for businesses of all sizes. Its strength lies in its ability to target specific audiences, scale efficiently, and deliver immediate results. Let's explore the unique advantages of paid advertising, its types, and its potential to accelerate your business growth.

Why Paid Ads Deliver Faster Results Than Organic Marketing

While organic marketing is excellent for long-term relationship building, achieving visibility and results can slowly take time. Competing in the crowded digital space, particularly in search engines, often requires consistent effort over months or even years.

In contrast, paid advertising delivers instant visibility. With a strategic budget and optimized ad campaigns, your business can appear at the top of search results, social media feeds, or relevant websites, providing a quicker return on investment (ROI). This immediate exposure drives traffic, leads, and sales from the campaign's launch.

The Spectrum of Paid Advertising: Search, Display, Social, and More

Paid advertising encompasses various formats, including search, display, and social media ads. Each offers unique strengths:

- **Search Ads:** Target users who are actively searching for your products or services.

- **Display Ads:** Build brand awareness by appearing on relevant websites.

- **Social Media Ads:** Leverage demographics, interests, and behaviors to deliver targeted messages.

A combined approach enhances the impact. For instance, you could start with search ads to reach high-intent users, reinforce your brand with display ads, and engage your audience further through social media campaigns.

Real-World ROI for Small Businesses

Paid advertising can yield impressive results for small and medium-sized businesses (SMBs). For example, a local bakery used Facebook ads to boost store visits by 30% in one month, while a small online retailer increased revenue by 50% within three months using Google Ads. These real-world examples highlight how paid advertising can drive rapid growth for businesses with limited budgets.

Higher Conversions From Paid Ads

Paid advertising often results in higher conversion rates. Unlike organic traffic, where users may browse without intent, paid ads target users actively searching for what you offer. Businesses can increase conversions by combining clear calls to action, engaging visuals, and intent-based targeting.

Building Wealth Through Strategic Advertising

Starting small with paid ads allows businesses to optimize campaigns over time. Even modest budgets can yield significant results when strategically managed. Paid advertising offers businesses the advantage of rapid growth while maintaining a competitive edge.

Looking Ahead: Mastering Google Ads

Now that you understand the power of paid advertising, it's time to dive deeper. In the next chapter, we'll explore Google Ads—a platform that connects you with audiences actively searching for your products or services. We'll cover keyword research, ad extensions, performance tracking, and remarketing strategies to help you maximize results.

Your business's bright future begins here. Together, let's master wealth and build the foundation for sustained growth and success.

About Sharyn Faison-Williams

Sharyn Faison-Williams is the founder and CEO of the anointed Grace Sixty Enterprise, Grace Sixty Marketing Agency, Team Leader in the Federal Government, Enlarging Your Circle of Love Ministry, and an author. She is a dedicated Seeds of Greatness Bible Church member and a covenant partner with Bill Winston Ministries. Known for her compassion and commitment, Sharyn finds joy in blessing others and serving her community.

At 60, Sharyn stepped out on faith to pursue her God-given calling, believing that her obedience would open doors for business owners in need. She often shares that she asks the Lord daily to let His Spirit guide her and considers it a privilege to fulfill her assignments. One of her missions is to help small and medium-sized businesses scale to extraordinary heights.

Sharyn is a devoted wife, mother of five adult children, and proud grandmother to her granddaughter, Kaliyah. When not working, she enjoys spending quality time with her family, planning special meals, reading, and baking. Her unwavering faith and commitment to serving others inspire all who cross her path.

NOTES

NOTES

NOTES

THE PURPOSE OF GRANTS & GOVERNMENT CONTRACTS TO SCALE

Dr. Michelle Walker-Davis

Did you know that $850 billion in grants and $8 trillion in government contracts are available yearly? That's $850 billion in FREE MONEY for small businesses, nonprofits, schools, communities, and church projects—funding that can help you expand, innovate, and transform your business without needing to pay it back.

Have you applied? If not, you're not alone. Many minority-owned businesses, women, veterans, Black churches, and minority-led nonprofits haven't applied. Why? Common reasons include:

- It takes too much time to apply or read the funding notices.

- Uncertainty about qualifying or responding to applications.

- Concerns over revenue requirements or government involvement.

- The process seems highly competitive, time-consuming and may require a professional.

While these challenges are real, remember that if you don't apply, someone else will potentially scale their business tenfold with the funds you could be using. The one sure thing: if you don't apply, you can't win.

By the end of this chapter, I hope to inspire you to join the "Money Team" and go after the millions available with your name on it!

The Difference between a Grant and a Government Contract

What is a Grant?

A grant is an award, usually financial, given by a company, foundation, or government to an individual or business:

- To support a specific goal or incentivize performance.

- Grants are essentially *free money*—gifts that do not have to be paid back.

Myth 1: It's free money; I can use it however I want!

Not true. Grants are typically designated for a specific program or project unless the funder specifies it as unrestricted. To be considered, you need a clearly outlined project plan with defined goals. Grant money cannot be used for general business growth, overhead costs, purchasing premises, or paying off business debts. Instead, it must be applied to a particular idea, project, product, or service. That's why the application process requires outlining exactly how every penny will be spent.

Myth 2: A grant proposal is easy to write—anyone can do it.

That's not true. Writing a compelling proposal can take days, sometimes up to 8 weeks or more for federal grants. Writing any grant proposal is hard work and requires significant time and effort. Starting the night before the deadline is unlikely to succeed.

Myth 3: It's all about who needs the money.

Not necessarily. Funders look for a return on their investment. They seek projects or programs that best align with their mission or cause. Applications require details, such as what the project entails, who will be involved, execution plans, why the funds are needed, and the project timeline.

What is a Government Contract?

A government contract is a formal, legally binding agreement between a government entity and a contractor. It involves two parties: a government entity (federal, state, or local) and a private business or individual. A contract can be used for various purposes, such as procurement of goods and services, construction projects, research, etc.

Competitive Bidding: Potential contractors often participate in a competitive bidding process, where they submit proposals outlining how they will fulfill the government's requirements and at what cost.

Terms and Conditions: Once awarded, the government contract specifies the terms, conditions, deliverables, and payment arrangements for the work.

Regulations and Oversight: Government contracts are subject to specific rules, regulations, and oversight to ensure fairness, transparency, and compliance with applicable laws and regulations

- It's an additional income stream.

- If you don't apply, you can't win.

- Once you win, more opportunities often follow.

- During COVID, the government provided billions to support small businesses and continues to offer billions in funding.

- Many micro-businesses didn't apply and missed out on this free money.

- Our clients received between $10,000 and $500,000 in COVID funding.

The Marketplace for Grants:

There is an enormous amount of grant money out there. Here is the breakdown of the $850B in grants awarded annually.

- **$550B** – Available from government sources: federal, state, and local (city, municipal, and county).

- **$250B** – Available from private foundations and philanthropists, such as Best Buy and MacArthur Foundation.

- **$50B** – Available from private corporations like BG&E, PSE&G, and Bank of America.

The Why Part I

Over $850B in grant funding is available. Overall, less than 4% were awarded to African Americans, Women, and the BIPOC community.

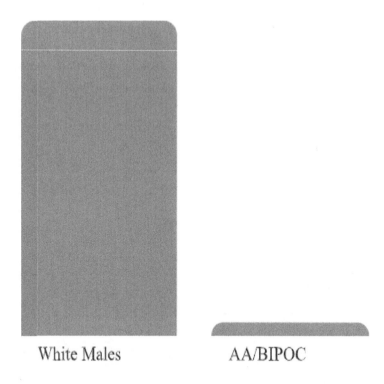

White Males   AA/BIPOC

The purpose of showing you this is to get you angry and motivated to apply. Once we enter anything, a sport, activity, or business venture, we usually get in, take it over, and win! It's your time. Let's Go!

The Why Part II

- Over $8 Trillion was awarded in government contracts. Only 1% awarded to Veterans.

- Only .006% awarded to African Americans, Women, and the BIPOC community overall.

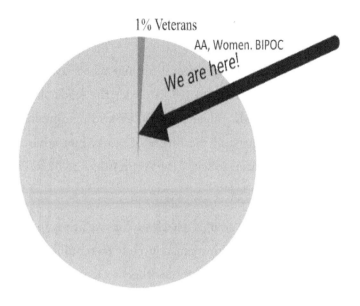

This greater share of the pie represents the 99% of awards won by white-male-owned businesses.

It's Time for Action!

Minority-owned businesses miss out on access to $8 trillion in government contracts each year. We can't continue letting others win by default. They know we aren't applying, so we aren't competing. It's time to level the playing field. It's time to accelerate your business and move from red to green! With millions in grants and government contracts, you can scale your business, close the wealth gap for Black-owned and women-owned firms, and compete effectively. Grants and contracts range from $500 to $5 million, often covering 3-to-5-year terms. Imagine the boost this could give your business!

More than ever, your purpose should be to use other people's money to scale your business. This funding is available to everyone — it's time to claim what's yours. Don't let others take the bulk of the funding simply because we're not in the game.

About Dr. Michelle Walker-Davis

Dr. Michelle Walker-Davis founded Imperial Management Group (IMG), specializing in grant development and government contracts for minority-owned businesses and nonprofits. She has developed award-winning proposals and secured over $50 million in funding from government, foundation, and industry sources.

As the Lead Associate for government funding access at Robert's Innovation Technology Institute, Dr. Walker-Davis works under the leadership of Dr. Michael V. Roberts, a Black billionaire who advances HBCUs and marginalized communities through technology, innovation, and the future of work. Her advisor is Dr. Randal Pinkett, the first African American to win "The Apprentice" at BCT Partners, a leader in tech and data innovation leader.

Dr. Walker-Davis's primary goal is to close the wealth gap for marginalized communities, using grants and government contracts to rebuild Black communities, empower women and girls globally, and enable others to achieve the American Dream.

Visit imgconsulting.info for more information on Imperial Management Group or to book Dr. Michelle Walker-Davis for a speaking engagement.

NOTES

NOTES

NOTES

THE PURPOSE OF UNVEILING HIDDEN TRUTHS

Sharon Cornelius

Introduction: The Reality of Wealth

When people talk about wealth, they often focus on the glamor, luxury, and freedom it brings. However, what's rarely discussed—and what I've learned through my journey—is the complex and often painful path that wealth demands. Becoming wealthy requires more than hard work and smart investments; it requires sacrifices, sleepless nights, and a resilience few are prepared for.

Unveiling Hidden Truths

Uncovering hidden truths about wealth is complex and transformative. It requires courage, introspection, and a willingness to confront uncomfortable realities. Successful people, including myself, often conceal specific struggles beneath polished exteriors. This chapter delves into the layers of these truths to provide a deeper understanding of the sacrifices, emotions, and dynamics that influence success.

The Facade of Perfection

Successful individuals craft an image of perfection, presenting material wealth, professional achievements, and flawless personal lives. For me, "fake it until you make it" was not just a mantra—it became my reality. Beneath the surface, however, there were struggles, insecurities, and unfulfilled desires. This disconnect between the external image and internal reality often forces you to live up to an ideal that isn't sustainable.

The Emotional Toll of Wealth

The sacrifices and emotional toll accompanying wealth are often left out of motivational speeches. The journey to financial success can feel isolating. Family and friends drift away, relationships become strained, and life's simple pleasures begin to feel like distractions. I remember the early days when I worked late into the night, long after everyone else had gone to bed. My social life dwindled, and I became increasingly isolated. While my peers enjoyed weekends, I was grinding, planning, and obsessing over every detail of my work. At the time, I told myself this was just the price of success. What I didn't realize was how much I was sacrificing emotionally.

The Cost of Sacrifices

Wealth often requires a single-minded focus that pushes everything else aside. Relationships suffer, and the people who once mattered feel like secondary characters in a story dominated by the pursuit of wealth. Without the right support system, this can be detrimental to mental health.

Another hidden truth is the weight of sacrifices. Becoming wealthy often means making hard choices that can feel impossible. One of the most brutal sacrifices for me was time with my husband, time for myself, and time just to be present. There were years when I missed essential moments in the lives of those I cared about because I was too busy chasing the next deal or working on the next project. Birthdays and anniversaries passed, and I told myself there would be time to make up for it later. But deep down, I knew some moments were lost forever, especially when loved ones passed unexpectedly.

The Role of Fear

Fear is another hidden truth. The fear of failure, of losing everything you've worked for, is a constant companion. This fear can be paralyzing, especially when you've experienced loss before and never want to return to that place. Fear drove me to work harder, take calculated risks, and stay ahead, but it also brought stress and anxiety. The higher you climb, the more you lose; that fear only grows.

Finding Purpose

As a married woman with no kids, I also encountered another profound truth—the question of purpose. Once I reached a certain level of financial success, I began to ask: Why am I doing this? What is all this wealth for? For years, I was driven by the desire to prove myself, but once I achieved my financial goals, I realized wealth in itself is not a purpose. It's a tool, not the end. Without a clear purpose, wealth can leave you feeling empty.

This realization shifted my focus. I began thinking about how to use my wealth to make a difference and create something lasting. This shift was not easy, but it was necessary. It helped me move beyond the narrow pursuit of financial success and find fulfillment in a more profound sense of purpose.

Conclusion: The Value of Hidden Truths

Ultimately, unveiling these hidden truths is not about discouraging the pursuit of wealth but providing an honest perspective. Wealth can bring freedom, security, and opportunity, but it also comes with challenges. Loneliness, sacrifices, fear, and the need for purpose are all part of the journey. Recognizing these truths helps shape the experience of becoming wealthy, influencing decisions, risks, and relationships.

In the end, wealth is not just about money. It's about the life you create, the impact you make, and the legacy you leave behind. To achieve true wealth—encompassing fulfillment, purpose, and peace—you must confront and embrace these hidden truths. These truths matter most because they guide you through challenges, help you make hard decisions, and keep you grounded in success. As you embark on your journey, look beyond the surface and consider the deeper realities. And don't forget to reach back and bring someone else along.

About Sharon Cornelius

Sharon Cornelius, Owner and Broker-in-Charge of SC Realty Columbia, has lived in Columbia her entire life and proudly serves the city and its surrounding areas. With over 28 years of real estate experience, Sharon is licensed in South Carolina, North Carolina, and Georgia.

Sharon is deeply involved in the real estate community and is committed to lifelong learning. She continuously takes courses and classes to expand her expertise in the industry. Sharon is a 2010 graduate of the prestigious South Carolina Leadership Program, a distinction awarded to fewer than 20 agents nationwide yearly.

Dedicated to giving back, Sharon volunteers her time to several charitable organizations. She is the only REALTOR® to have served on all Central Carolina REALTORS® Association committees and as a Director on the Board of REALTORS®. In 2012, she served as Secretary for the Central Carolina REALTORS® Association Board of Directors.

Sharon is also a member of The National Association of Real Estate Brokers (NAREB), a 2024 graduate of the Black Developers Academy, and an active participant in the United Developers Council (UDC). Additionally, she holds numerous certifications, including Real Estate Probate Specialist, and is currently developing single-family homes in South Carolina. For more information, visit: SharonCornelius.Com

NOTES

NOTES

NOTES

CONCLUSION: MASTERING WEALTH

As we conclude *Mastering Wealth: Volume 2 Purpose*, it becomes clear that wealth is far more than a number in a bank account—it's a multifaceted journey that integrates financial understanding, personal growth, and a deep sense of purpose. The chapters in this book have showcased a broad spectrum of strategies and philosophies, each contributing a unique perspective on what it means to build, sustain, and leverage wealth in a way that creates a lasting impact.

From Percy "Master P" Miller's exploration of philanthropy as a vehicle for transformative change to Tiana Von Johnson's lessons on branding your brilliance, this book has shown that wealth is not confined to financial gain but extends to the power of giving, storytelling, and inspiring others. Whether through the thoughtful application of *Other People's Money* by Dr. Rosie Thomas or the role of *Life Insurance* as a cornerstone of generational wealth by Tony R. Jackson, each chapter underscores the importance of using wealth-building tools strategically to create a legacy.

The contributors have also emphasized the human side of wealth: Reginald K. Harris's exploration of emotional resilience, MiaMichelle Henry's sharing of deep healing and purpose in grief, and Phyllis Utley's emphasis on the critical role of family history. These chapters remind us that mastering wealth is more about personal growth and emotional intelligence than financial strategies.

Education and empowerment are central themes throughout this book, whether through Lisa Watson's call for Black-owned K-12 education, Dr. Ruby Mendenhall's vision for training youth as healers, or LaToshia Hall's guidance on building generational wealth through real estate. These contributions reflect the necessity of creating systems that uplift individuals and entire communities.

In addition to strategy and insight, this book challenges readers to confront personal and societal barriers. Aaron W. Smith's exploration of curbing emotional spending and Sharon Cornelius's perspective on unveiling hidden truths encourage us to look inward and examine the habits and beliefs that may limit our success. Together with the insights shared by all the contributing authors, these lessons are essential for moving beyond surface-level solutions to achieve a deeper understanding of wealth and purpose.

As you close this book, consider the opportunities to achieve financial success and create a legacy that resonates far beyond your lifetime. Wealth can transform lives, families, and communities when aligned with purpose. It is a tool to break cycles of poverty, challenge stereotypes, and lay the foundation for generational prosperity.

The path to mastering wealth is not a singular journey but a collective effort. As you apply the lessons from this book, remember that your success is not only for your benefit but for the empowerment of those who follow in your footsteps. Together, through intentional action and purpose-driven decisions, we can redefine what wealth means and ensure that its impact extends far beyond ourselves.

This is your call to action—to take what you've learned, to dream bigger, and to make a difference. The journey to wealth mastery begins and ends with purpose. Let this be your guiding principle as you step forward into a future of abundance, fulfillment, and lasting impact.

Made in the USA
Columbia, SC
09 December 2024

47641570R10111